DUMBO

THE LITTLE
MERMAID

FANTASIA

"Melody Time"

Pinocchio

SILLY SYMPHONY

The Music Of Disney

A Legacy In Song

Table Of Contents

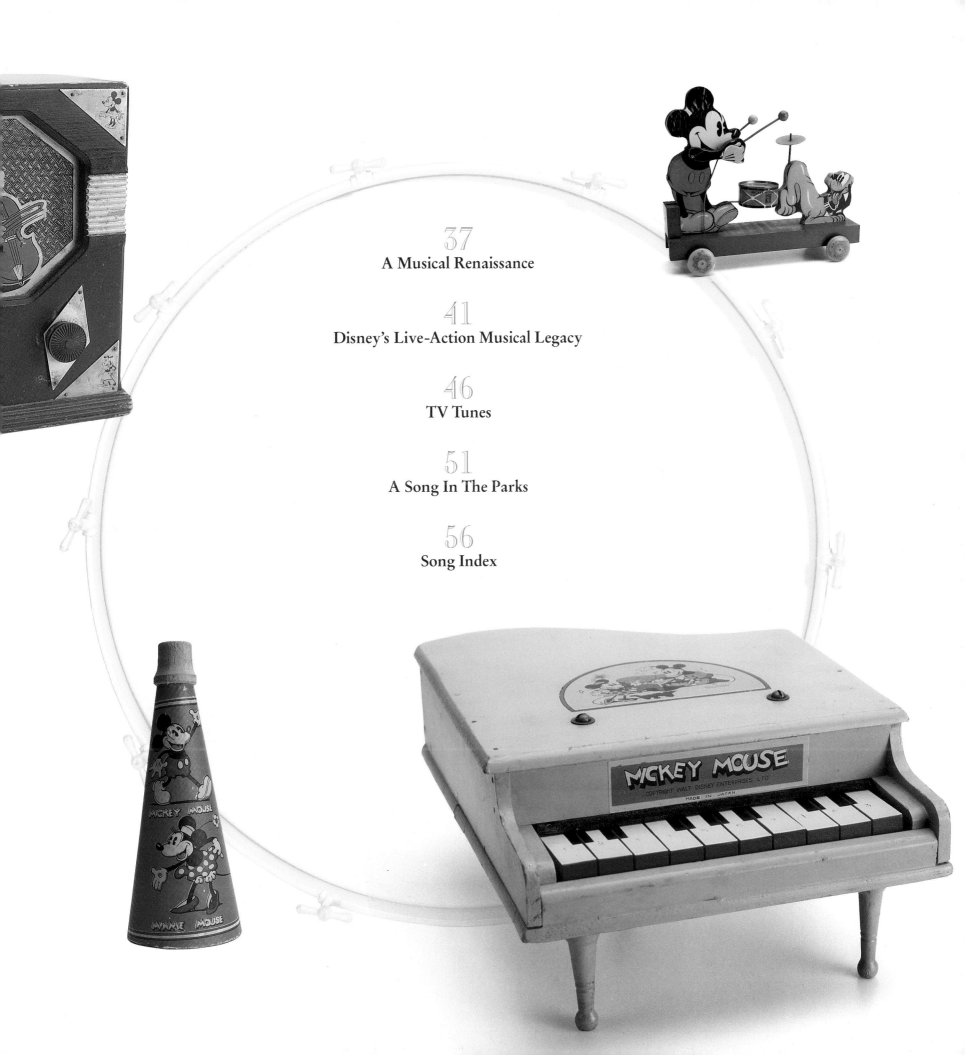

Introduction

Walt and Roy Disney with the special "Oscar" awarded to Walt in 1932 for the creation of Mickey Mouse.

Walt Disney didn't read or write music. In fact, he never even played an instrument. And yet his influence upon music was and continues to be so profound that the great American composer Jerome Kern was moved to say, "Disney has made use of music as language. In the synchronization of humorous episodes with humorous music, he has unquestionably given us the outstanding contribution of our time."

That's obviously lofty praise, especially coming as it did from a musical legend like Kern. But what makes his words all the more amazing is the fact that he said them in 1936, before the release of *Snow White and the Seven Dwarfs,* which is arguably not only one of Walt Disney's greatest moments in animation, but in music as well.

Still, the question remains: if Walt didn't write any songs or compose any scores, how could he have had such a deep and lasting impact on music?

The answer, simply enough, is the same way in which he had such a profound effect upon animation without actually animating even one mouse or dwarf.

Walt was the mover and shaker, the man of vision who gathered around him some of the most talented writers, artists, composers and musicians who bought into his dreams and schemes and made them happen, all under his watchful eye.

"There's a terrific power to music. You can run any of these pictures and they'd be dragging and boring, but the minute you put music behind them, they have life and vitality they don't get any other way."

Walt Disney

5

Disney's imprimatur is stamped onto every song...

Music lightens a story session in the mid-1930's as Walt Disney visits (from left) Webb Smith, Ted Sears and Pinto Colvig.

"Cartoonist Walt Disney has made the twentieth century's only important contribution to music. Disney has made use of music as language."

Jerome Kern

He once described his role this way:

My role? Well, you know I was stumped one day when a little boy asked, "Do you draw Mickey Mouse?" I had to admit I do not draw anymore. "Then you think up the jokes and ideas?" "No," I said, "I don't do that." Finally, he looked at me and said, "Mr. Disney, just what do you do?" "Well," I said, "sometimes I think of myself as a little bee. I go from one area of the Studio to another and gather pollen and sort of stimulate everybody. I guess that's the job I do."

Of course, that doesn't explain Walt Disney's uncanny feel for what worked and what didn't, be it in music, films or theme parks.

Perhaps Eric Sevareid summed it up best in his tribute to Walt on the "CBS Evening News" the day Walt died: "He was an original; not just an American original, but an original, period. He was a happy accident; one of the happiest this century has experienced… People are saying we'll never see his like again."

Maybe it was his Midwestern upbringing and mid-American, mainstream appreciation for music and movies, or maybe he was just "a happy accident," but Walt Disney aimed to create entertainment that he himself would enjoy. Could he help it if hundreds of millions of people around the world happened to agree with him?

So although he didn't write "When You Wish Upon a Star," "Zip-A-Dee-Doo-Dah" or any of the other hundreds of tunes that make up the Disney canon, his imprimatur is stamped onto every song and score. When you hear "Whistle While You Work," you may not know that the words were written by Larry Morey and the music by Frank Churchill, but you certainly know it's a Disney song.

Disney songs represent a style and sprightliness that makes them eminently hummable and totally unforgettable. They were very much a reflection of their patron, who concentrated on melody and didn't like anything that was too loud or high-pitched.

Portrait of Walt Disney in 1944 by renowned Hollywood photographer George Hurrell.

Even the "Disney" songs and scores being written today, a whole quarter of a century after Walt Disney's death, reflect the spirit and influence of this man who had a special ability to recognize what kind of music best fit a scene or situation and, more importantly (and more to the point), what was good.

It was Walt's direction and influence that led his composers and musicians to pioneer musical concepts and technologies that influenced both the film and music industries for decades—and continue to do so to this day.

The Music of Disney: A Legacy in Song contains a representative sampling of songs from Disney films, television shows and theme parks, from the beginnings of the Disney Studio on into today. The music embraces a wide range of themes and styles, and indicates the breadth and depth of the Disney music library.

The songs for this collector's edition were selected after months of research, debate and difficult decision-making. Such is the dilemma when you have so much excellent music to choose from but only three CDs or tapes to put it on. However, it is our hope that the songs we have selected—78 of them representing over three hours of music—will bring back many warm memories or, for those in the early years of life, create some new ones.

So sit back, relax and we'll share with you more than 60 years of Disney music. Along the way, you'll hear some time-honored classics, a few obscure but no less noteworthy tunes and, best of all, just some plain good music.

(Top) Walt Disney's classic portrait with Mickey Mouse, taken at the Disney Studios on Hyperion Avenue in the 1930s. (Right) In 1938, Disney purchased undeveloped property in Burbank, which soon became the permanent home to the new Walt Disney Studios.

Walt Disney aimed to create entertainment that he himself would enjoy

The Early Years

"**T**urkey in the Straw" seems to be a strange way to begin the Disney musical legacy. Possibly of Irish origin (though no one seems to know for sure who wrote it or when), it is one of those sing-song classics that has endured due to the fact it's both catchy and simple. Let's face it, we're not talking Beethoven's Fifth Symphony or Vivaldi's *Four Seasons* here; it's more like "Camptown Races" or "My Darling Clementine."

In any case, it's significant because it's not only one of the first songs to be heard in a Disney cartoon (in this case, Mickey Mouse's 1928 debut, *Steamboat Willie*), it's one of the first songs to be heard in any cartoon (or at least any cartoon where the sound is synchronized with the action).

(Here's one for you trivia buffs: the first song to be heard in a Disney cartoon, and thus a cartoon with synchronized sound, was "Steamboat

In 1929, the Disney Studios' creative team included (standing from left) John Cannon, Walt Disney, Bert Gillett, Ub Iwerks, Wilfred Jackson, Les Clark; (seated from left) Carl Stalling, Jack King and Ben Sharpsteen.

The sound that played the key role in Disney cartoons was music

Bill," which played over the opening credits and first scene of *Steamboat Willie*.)

The fact that there's sound and music at all in *Steamboat Willie* is an early testament to Walt Disney's vision and genius. At that time, talking pictures were a novelty. *The Jazz Singer* had debuted in 1927, but many Hollywood studio chiefs considered sound nothing more than a passing fancy.

Walt did not share their opinion. He was one of the first to buy into and experiment with sound, which he saw as a way to not only launch his new Mickey Mouse character, but also as a key to keeping his struggling young studio afloat.

From the start, the sound that played the key role in Disney cartoons was music. In *Steamboat Willie*, the characters don't actually talk; they just sort of squeak, squawk and grunt. The real innovation comes musically, first with Mickey whistling "Steamboat Bill" and then later when he rigs up a goat as a hurdy-gurdy and begins playing **"Turkey in the Straw."** (Mickey also manages to play a washboard, pots and pans, a cat, a duck, several suckling pigs and a cow's teeth, which should go a long way in explaining all the strange noises heard during the song.)

The credit (or the blame) for the use of "Turkey in the Straw" goes to a young assistant animator named Wilfred Jackson, who went on to become a leading animator and animation director at the Disney Studio.

When Walt was conducting early experiments into whether sound could be synchronized with animation,

Mickey Mouse and the musical improvisation that made him famous in his debut film, Steamboat Willie.

In the Mickey cartoons, the music would continue to play second fiddle to the characters and the action, but in the "Silly Symphonies" the music would rule.

However, Stalling stayed with the Studio for only two years, jumping from "Silly Symphonies" at Disney to "Looney Tunes" and "Merrie Melodies" at Warner Brothers, where he created his own musical legacy by composing scores for Bugs Bunny, Daffy Duck and Porky Pig, among others.

Realizing the increasing importance of music to his cartoons, especially with the advent of the "Silly Symphony" series, Walt Disney began beefing up his music staff in the early 1930s. One of the composers he hired was Frank Churchill, a young musician who had studied at UCLA and gained his experience playing honky-tonk piano in Mexico and performing on a Los Angeles radio station (as well as serving as a session player in recording sessions for Disney cartoons). This heretofore unsung musician would play an important role in Disney music over the next decade. And he started off with a bang, writing Disney's first big hit, a song that came out of the most famous of the "Silly Symphonies," *Three Little Pigs*.

Released in 1933 during the depths of the Depression, *Three Little Pigs* and its famous song, **"Who's Afraid of the Big Bad Wolf?"**, provided hope and humor to a country that was badly in need of both.

e called on Jackson who, as a harmonica player, was the sole musician at the small Disney Studio. ackson knew only a few simple tunes on the armonica and his favorite was—surprise!— "Turkey in the Straw."

And thus began, humbly enough, the Disney musical legacy.

Fortunately, from then on Walt Disney entrusted his music to his own tastes and more accomplished musicians, including his first musical director, Carl Stalling, an old friend from Kansas City who began by scoring the music to the next two Mickey Mouse cartoon shorts, *Gallopin' Gaucho* and *Plane Crazy*. (*Gallopin' Gaucho* and *Plane Crazy* were actually created before *Steamboat Willie*, but were held for release until sound could be added to them.)

It was Stalling who persuaded Walt to begin the "Silly Symphonies" cartoon series, which produced a host of firsts for the Disney Studio, including the use of color and the multi-plane camera, and the first hit song. The series grew out of disagreements Walt and Stalling had over the use of music in the Mickey Mouse shorts. Walt wanted Stalling to fit the music to the action, while Stalling felt the action should fit the music.

The compromise was the "Silly Symphonies."

"Who's Afraid of the Big Bad Wolf?" provided hope and humor to a country that was badly in need of both.

The surprise hit song from Three Little Pigs *spawned a range of merchandise, including (left to right) sheet music, a board game, and records. These rare 1933 items are treasured by collectors today.*

9

While this "Silly Symphony" became a huge box office success (and perhaps the most popular cartoon of all time), the song became a hit in its own right, topping the Hit Parade for several weeks in 1933 and selling several million copies to an American public that adopted the tune as a cheery anthem for the dark days of the Depression.

As with many Disney films, *Three Little Pigs* comes from a children's story. But to Churchill, it also represented real life. While growing up on his family's ranch in San Luis Obispo, California, he was given three piglets to raise by his mother. All went well until a real "Big Bad Wolf" killed one of them.

As legend has it, when Churchill was asked to write a song for the cartoon, he recalled his horrifying childhood experience and penned "Who's Afraid of the Big Bad Wolf?" in about five

minutes, patterning the song loosely on "Happy Birthday." Ted Sears, a writer in the story department, wrote the lyrics.

Interestingly, the song is never heard in its entirety during the cartoon. The version that was released on record was recorded after *Three Little Pigs* was released and features additional lyrics by Ann Ronell.

Also, if the voice of Practical Pig sounds a bit Goofy, that's because it is. Pinto Colvig, the man responsible for Practical Pig, also provided the original voice for Goofy.

Three Little Pigs won an Academy Award for Best Cartoon Short Subject for 1933, but "Who's Afraid of the Big Bad Wolf?" was never considered for an award. The reason was simple enough: Best Song did not become part of the Academy Awards until the following year.

Walt Disney visits as Mary Moder, Pinto Colvig and Dorothy Compton rehearse "Who's Afraid of the Big Bad Wolf?" under the direction of Frank Churchill (at piano) in 1933.

A Coming Of Age

he story of *Snow White and the Seven Dwarfs* is well known and well documented: Walt Disney gambles the future of his studio on an expensive, lavishly drawn full-length animated feature. Skeptics dub the movie "Disney's folly," claiming no one will sit through an 83-minute cartoon. The film is released just before Christmas in 1937 and becomes a runaway box office success, not to mention one of the greatest movies of all time.

But what is not so well known is that Walt had much more in mind than "just" creating and producing the first animated feature. What he envisioned was something closer to Broadway musical than Hollywood motion picture.

From its beginnings, *Snow White* was planned around music. Unfortunately, early attempts at songs for the movie did not satisfy Walt. He

"We should set a new pattern, a new way to use music"

complained that they were too much in the vein of so many Hollywood musicals, which introduced songs and dances without regard to the story. "We should set a new pattern, a new way to use music," he told his staff during the early stages of production. "Weave it into the story so somebody doesn't just burst into song."

Frustration must have run rampant through the Disney music department during the production of *Snow White* because by the time all was said and sung, Frank Churchill and a young artist named Larry Morey (who also served as a sequence director on the movie) had written 25 songs, only eight of which ended up in the film, but what an eight they were.

Walt didn't write a single note of music or contribute any lyrics (or at least he didn't take credit for any), but he was the one who defined the content of each song and how it fit into the film. His intense involvement is detailed in these notes from a story conference in which he is discussing the use of **"Whistle While You Work"** in the film:

Change words of song so they fit in more with Snow White's handing the animals brushes, etc. Snow White: "If you just hum a merry tune"... and they start humming. Then Snow White would start to tell them to "whistle while you work." She would start giving the animals things to do. By that time, she has sung, of course... Birds would

Composer Frank Churchill (left) and sequence director/lyricist Larry Morey in the mid-1930s creating songs for Snow White and the Seven Dwarfs.

come marching in. Try to arrange to stay with the birds for a section of whistling. Orchestra would play with a whistling effect... get it in the woodwinds... like playing something instrumentally to sound like whistling...

Get a way to finish the song that isn't just an end. Work in a shot trucking [moving] out of the house. Truck back and show animals shaking rugs out of the windows... little characters outside beating things out in the yard...

Truck out and the melody of "Whistle While You Work" gets quieter and quieter. Leave them all working. The last thing you see as you truck away is little birds hanging out clothes. Fade out on that and music would fade out. At the end, all you would hear is the flute—before fading into the "Dig Dig" song [which precedes the song "Heigh-Ho"] and the hammering rhythm.

Eighteen-year-old Adriana Caselotti, who was trained in Italian opera, provided Snow White's beautiful, tender soprano, which is heard in "Whistle While You Work" and **"Someday My Prince Will Come."**

Chanting their way through **"Heigh-Ho"** as the dwarfs were vaudeville comic Roy Atwell as Doc, comedian Billy Gilbert as Sneezy, Scotty Mattraw as Bashful, Otis Harlan as Happy and the irrepressible and invaluable Pinto Colvig as both Grumpy and Sleepy. In case you're wondering why only six dwarfs are listed, remember, Dopey never speaks.

Perhaps more astounding than the success of the movie was the chart performance of the songs featured in it. In fact, more popular hit songs

Snow White and friends celebrate in the world's first feature length animated film, Snow White and the Seven Dwarfs.

originated with *Snow White and the Seven Dwarfs* than any other Disney animated film. *The Hit Parade* of 1938 featured six tunes from the film: the three included in this collection, as well as "One Song," "With a Smile and a Song" and "I'm Wishing."

Come Academy Awards time, though, the film and its songs were almost completely overlooked. The score, by Disney music staffers Leigh Harline, Frank Churchill and Paul J. Smith, was nominated for an award, thanks in part to a new rule that guaranteed every studio at least one nomination in the Best Score category simply by submitting an entry.

As for Best Song, not one of *Snow White's* eight songs was nominated, but at least they were in good company. Such classics as "Hooray for Hollywood" and "Let's Call the Whole Thing Off" also failed to receive nominations, which left the Oscar to something called "Sweet Leilani" from the movie *Waikiki Wedding.*

(*Snow White and the Seven Dwarfs* did earn a special Oscar; in fact, it earned one Oscar and seven little Oscars, which were presented to Walt Disney by Shirley Temple. The award recognized *Snow White* "as a significant screen innovation which has charmed millions and pioneered a great new entertainment field for the motion picture cartoon.")

In 1939, Walt Disney received a special full-size "Oscar" and seven miniatures from Shirley Temple for his achievements in creating Snow White and the Seven Dwarfs.

It didn't take long for the Academy of Motion Picture Arts and Sciences to make up for its transgression in almost completely ignoring the music in *Snow White and the Seven Dwarfs.* Disney's next film, *Pinocchio,* released in early 1940, took two of the three music awards at the 1941 Academy Awards, earning Oscars for Best Song (**"When You Wish Upon a Star"**) and Best Original Score (the third music category was Best Adapted Score, for which *Pinocchio* was not eligible).

The success of *Pinocchio's* songs and score provided some consolation for Walt since the movie itself was a money loser in its initial release (thanks largely to World War II, which succeeded in shutting off Disney's foreign markets, markets that usually accounted for almost half of the company's income). Of course, the movie later became a roaring financial success in subsequent rereleases and on videocassette.

The two Academy Awards also served to vindicate Walt after several reviewers complained that the songs in *Pinocchio* were not as good as those in *Snow White.*

"What they [the critics] failed to realize," wrote Maurice Sendak in the *Los Angeles Times* upon the film's rerelease in 1978, "is that the score is a vital, integral part of the whole; nothing was allowed to obtrude, even at the risk of sacrificing obvious melody and the hit song charts."

And yet Walt and his writers, Ned Washington and Leigh Harline, ended up sacrificing neither melody nor the song charts. Upon its release, "When You Wish Upon a Star" broke all *Hit Parade* records and has gone on to become the most beloved of all Disney tunes. For years, it was the opening song for Disney's network television show and it's heard every night at closing in both Disneyland and the Magic Kingdom at Walt Disney World.

Cliff Edwards, who had a hit song in the 1920s as a character called "Ukulele Ike," provided the voice for Jiminy Cricket, the official, 18-karat conscience of Pinocchio who croons "When You Wish Upon a Star" and **"Give a Little Whistle,"** the two songs from the film

included in this collection (in "Give a Little Whistle," he gets a little help from 12-year-old Dickie Jones, who, because he had "a typical nice boy voice," landed the role of Pinocchio).

Walt Disney met Leopold Stokowski, the famed conductor of the Philadelphia Orchestra, by chance at a restaurant in the late 1930s. A big fan of Disney cartoons, Stokowski expressed an interest in working with his newfound friend. Walt responded that perhaps he could use Stokowski's expertise immediately because his studio was currently working on a version of Paul Dukas' "The Sorcerer's Apprentice" with Mickey Mouse in the title role.

Stokowski eagerly agreed to conduct the music for the short and, after a visit to the studio, suggested that Walt tackle an entire feature composed of sequences animated to popular classical music. Walt agreed and *Fantasia* was born ("fantasia," by the way, is a musical term meaning the free development of a composition or theme).

Walt wasn't aiming for an audience of stuffed shirts with *Fantasia*. Nor was he trying to educate common folk in the ways of highbrow culture. To him, the film was simply another challenge in his continuing effort to push the boundaries of animation.

Some music critics reacted hostilely to the film. They objected to both the adaptations of the scores (one critic called them "butchery") and their animated visualizations, which the purists decried because they felt listeners should create their own images for the music.

But even the film's harshest critics had to admit that *Fantasia* was completely different from anything they'd seen before. Instead of the music advancing the story, as had been the case in *Snow White* and *Pinocchio*, the music was the story. In that respect, *Fantasia* was essentially a series of music videos—and we know the debate that rages around them today (although, granted, what Walt and Stokowski had in mind wasn't anywhere near Madonna or Michael Jackson).

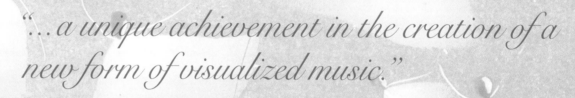

"…a unique achievement in the creation of a new form of visualized music."

Despite all the controversy over *Fantasia*, the film was still honored with two special Academy Awards for 1941, one for the innovative Fantasound system that was developed for the film and the other for Stokowski, who got some measure of revenge on his critics by being recognized for his "unique achievement in the creation of a new form of visualized music… thereby widening the scope of the motion picture as entertainment and art form."

Of course, the film and its music earned further redemption—and even some long overdue (albeit still grudgingly given) praise—when, after its first unsuccessful runs in the 1940s and 1950s, it gained new life during its releases in the 1970s and 1980s.

Walt Disney and Leopold Stokowski review music for Fantasia *in 1940.*

Original half-sheet movie poster from Dumbo, *as seen by theatergoers nationwide in 1941.*

In 1991 it became one of the biggest selling videocassettes of all time. The remastered soundtrack has also enjoyed great success, earning a gold record for sales of more than 500,000 copies.

The section of the score heard here, **"Dance of the Reed Flutes,"** comes from the *The Nutcracker Suite,* written by Peter Ilich Tchaikovsky. While listening to it, imagine delicate flower petals caught by the breeze, then gliding down to float amongst lily pads resting gently on water. At least that's the scenario imagined by Disney animators. Perhaps you'll think of something else.

With *Dumbo* and *Bambi,* Walt Disney returned to more conventional storytelling and musical scores, and he was rewarded both critically and commercially.

Dumbo hit the screens first, debuting in 1941 with six songs written by lyricist Ned Washington and composers Frank Churchill and Oliver Wallace. None of the songs from the film repeated the Hit Parade success of *Snow White* and *Pinocchio,* but the score earned Churchill and Wallace an Academy Award for Best Scoring of a Musical Picture and **"Baby Mine"** was nominated for Best Song. The Oscar that year went to "The Last Time I Saw Paris," which, ironically enough,

was co-written by Jerome Kern, the songwriter who said such nice things about Walt Disney just a few years earlier ("Baby Mine" was in good company, though: "Boogie Woogie Bugle Boy of Company B" and "Chattanooga Choo-Choo" also came up on the short end for Best Song).

Written by Churchill and Washington, "Baby Mine" is such a heartfelt ballad that tears are almost certainly guaranteed. In a gently humorous way, Steven Spielberg paid homage to the song in his movie *1941,* which featured General Joseph Stilwell, played by Robert Stack, crying as he watches Mrs. Jumbo try to comfort her poor son Dumbo.

Bambi also featured an Academy Award-nominated tune, **"Love Is a Song,"** but it, too, came up short at the awards ceremony. No one was surprised, though, since the winner for 1942 was a little ditty by Irving Berlin called "White Christmas." The score was also nominated,

*Although **Bambi** is a 69-minute film, it has less than 900 words of dialog (shorter than a four-page business letter). Clearly, music had to convey emotions and experiences that words could not.*

in the Best Scoring of a Dramatic or Comedy Picture category.

Churchill and Larry Morey, the duo behind the eight classic tunes that make up *Snow White and the Seven Dwarfs,* reteamed to write the songs for *Bambi,* a film that had been in development at the Disney Studio since 1935 (animation actually began in 1937, but the movie was constantly pushed aside in favor of other projects, such as *Pinocchio* and *Fantasia*). It was finally finished and released in 1942.

This time Churchill and Morey wrote four songs, including **"Little April Shower"** and the aforementioned "Love Is a Song."

As usual, Walt Disney was intimately involved in the development of the songs and the score, as evidenced by the reminiscences of two of Disney's top animators, Frank Thomas and Ollie Johnston, in their book *Disney Animation: The Illusion of Life:*

One day [Walt] was called into a meeting on the forest fire sequence in *Bambi,* just as he finished viewing the work reels on Beethoven's *Pastoral Symphony.*

The *Bambi* picture reel was only half completed, but the intent was clear and the musician, Ed Plumb [who collaborated with Churchill on the background music], was eager to present his ideas on the score he was writing.

Halfway through his presentation, Walt stopped him and asked the projectionist if the *Fantasia* reels were still up

"We were stunned by the power of the music…"

in the booth. They were, so he asked to hear the storm music from the *Pastoral Symphony* run in sync with the *Bambi* reel. We were stunned by the power of the music and the excitement it gave to the drawings.

When it was over, Walt turned and said, "There Ed. That's what I want. Something big. See the difference?"

Ed's look was part shock, part disbelief and part pleading. "But Walt—that's Beethoven!"

Walt responded, "Yeah…?" and waited to hear some reason why Ed could not write the same sort of thing.

Walt Disney reviews animation sketches for Bambi.

Expanding The Dream

In mid-1941, with war raging in Europe but the United States not yet involved, Nelson Rockefeller, the Coordinator of Inter-American Affairs for the State Department, asked Walt Disney and members of his staff to embark on a goodwill tour of South America. The reasons for the trip were two-fold: On the one hand, sending a much beloved figure like Walt would help the U.S.'s Good Neighbor Policy, which was designed to quell any pro-Axis feeling that existed south of the border. On the other hand, South America represented an untapped market for Hollywood motion picture studios such as Disney that were suffering from the loss of European revenues due to the war.

The results of the trip south were two travelog-style films combining live-action glimpses of South American culture with several cartoon sequences.

The first of the two films, *Saludos Amigos*, was released in 1943 and featured such Latin standards as "Tico Tico" and "Brazil." The one song written especially for the film, **"Saludos Amigos,"** was penned by Ned Washington and Charles Wolcott, who admitted prior to the trip that "my only exposure to Latin music was the sound of Xavier Cugat."

Apparently, the public and the Academy of Motion Picture Arts and Sciences liked what

South America represented an untapped market for Hollywood

Donald Duck takes a vacation and meets new friends in Saludos Amigos.

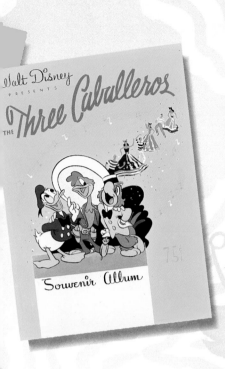

Gilbert-penned **"You Belong to My Heart"** which featured the vocal talents of Latin American singing star Dora Luz.

Perhaps no other song in the Disney pantheon has enjoyed greater popularity than **"Zip-A-Dee-Doo-Dah,"** the irresistibly bouncy, upbeat tune from *Song of the South* that has become nothing less than an anthem for happiness. Written by Allie Wrubel and Ray Gilbert, "Zip-A-Dee-Doo-Dah" not only topped the *Hit Parade* in 1946, it took home the Oscar for Best Song.

But the song's already considerable success hasn't ended there. It has become an enduring standard, popping up in the strangest places with performances by the most surprising of people. Producer Phil

Saludos Amigos was the first of several films that combined animation, live action and music. It also served as a quiet entry into live-action filmmaking.

isney's south-of-the-border films coincided with America's romance with Latin rhythms. it tunes found their way into record albums nd music folios in the 1940s and remained opular, as evidenced by the 1958 Disneyland ecords release (at left).

they saw and heard. The movie was a box office success both north and south of the border, while "Saludos Amigos" was nominated for Best Song and the score, composed by such Disney stalwarts as Ed Plumb, aul J. Smith and Wolcott, was nominated for est Scoring of a Musical Picture.

The second of the two Latin American-hemed movies was *The Three Caballeros*, vhich featured Donald Duck, Joe Carioca and new character, Panchito, on a musical romp hrough Mexico and South America.

Of the nine songs written for the film, two ecame hits: "Baia" and the Agustin Lara–Ray

Walt Disney talks with children working as extras during the filming of The Three Caballeros.

JAMES BASKETT

In 1945, James Baskett was playing fast-talking lawyer Gabby Gibson on the "Amos 'n' Andy" radio show when he answered an ad to provide the voice of a butterfly in Disney's Song of the South.

Not only did he get the part of the butterfly, he also got the lead role of Uncle Remus, served as the voice of the wily and conniving Brer Fox (a rather abrupt turnabout from his portrayal of the kindly Uncle Remus) and, as if all those roles weren't enough, also provided some of Brer Rabbit's vocalizations when Johnny Lee was called off on a USO tour in the middle of recording.

So Baskett went from one small role in Song of the South *to just about taking over the whole motion picture. Pretty good for a Midwestern kid who at one time studied to be a pharmacist before pursuing his first love, the theater.*

Completing this success story was the special Academy Award Baskett received in 1948 for his "able and heartwarming characterization" of Uncle Remus.

Alas, the euphoria was short-lived. Baskett died of a heart ailment just a few months after the Academy Awards ceremony.

Spector gave "Zip-A-Dee-Doo-Dah" his trademark "wall of sound" treatment in 1962 and turned it into a Top 10 hit on the Billboard pop chart for Bob B. Soxx and the Blue Jeans. The song has even turned up in other movies. For instance, in the 1984 hit *Splash*, Tom Hanks turns in an offhanded performance of "Zip-A-Dee-Doo-Dah" after spending a wild night with Daryl Hannah's mermaid character.

Somewhat lost in the hubbub over "Zip-A-Dee-Doo-Dah" was another toe-tapping ditty written for *Song of the South*, **"Ev'rybody Has a Laughing Place."** Also written by Wrubel and Gilbert, "Laughin' Place" is sung by Johnny Lee as Brer Rabbit with a little "help" from Nicodemus Stewart as Brer Bear.

In the mid-1940s, the Disney Studio released a number of "package" pictures, movies that featured a series of animated shorts rolled into one film. The impetus behind the movies was both personal and practical. On the personal side, Walt Disney had always wanted to do a sequel to *Fantasia*, but

"Zip - A - Dee - Doo - Dah"

on the practical side, the cost of producing such a film (not to mention the unlikelihood of making any money off of it, given the lack of success of that first effort) made such another ambitious undertaking an impossibility, especially considering the precarious financial position of the Disney Studio at that time.

So he made a compromise. Rather than use classical music for these pictures, which he thought might scare people away, he chose mainstream songs and popular performers as a means of enhancing each movie's box office appeal. The results were four features—*Make Mine Music* (1946), *Fun and Fancy Free* (1947), *Melody Time* (1948) and *The Adventures of Ichabod and Mr. Toad* (1949)—composed of fanciful music sequences. Call them an early version of DTV.

21

(Opposite) Bobby Driscoll, James ⸏askett and Luana Patten are ⸏ned by Brer Bear, Brer Rabbit ⸏d Brer Fox in Song of the ⸏uth. (Right) Brer Bear en route to ⸏re adventures with Brer Rabbit ⸏ the 1946 film.

Among the performers Walt called on were such popular recording artists as the Andrews Sisters, Jerry Colonna, Nelson Eddy, Benny Goodman, Dinah Shore, Roy Rogers, Fred Waring and the Sons of the Pioneers, and Freddy Martin and His Orchestra. Alas, despite the presence of these stars, none of the films did particularly well with either critics or audiences. However, they did produce some good music, including **"The Lord Is Good to Me,"** featured as part of "Johnny Appleseed" in *Melody Time*. Written by Kim Gannon and Walter Kent, the song is performed by Dennis Day and continues to be sung by children today, few of whom realize that it originated in a Disney film.

So Dear to My Heart, released in 1949, has long been considered one of Walt Disney's personal favorites. "*So Dear* was especially close to me," he once said in an interview. "That's the life my brother and I grew up with as kids out in Missouri."

The movie, a somewhat forgotten musical period piece that tells the story of a boy and his pet lamb, was the last step Walt took before releasing his first entirely live-action motion picture, *Treasure Island*, in 1950. In fact, some critics complained that the few, brief animated sequences actually intrude on what is a nice, understated film.

As is the case with many Disney movies, a large part of the movie's charm is derived from its music. In this case, it's several folk-inspired songs, among them **"Lavender Blue (Dilly, Dilly),"** sung by Burl Ives, who plays Uncle Hiram in the movie. "Lavender Blue," written by Eliot Daniel with lyrics by the ever-present Larry Morey, received an Academy Award nomination.

"So Dear was especially close to me. Why, that's the life my brother and I grew up with as kids out in Missouri."

Walt Disney

Burl Ives gives co-stars Bobby Driscoll and Luana Patten a lift in So Dear to My Heart.

22

Songs From Tin Pan Alley

The release of *Cinderella* in 1950 marked Walt Disney's return to feature-length animation after an absence of almost a decade, and it also represented two milestones in the way he produced music for his animated films.

The first was his decision to use pop songwriters outside the Disney stable to pen the movie's six tunes. He continued to depend on his staff for the musical direction and scores (in the case of *Cinderella*, it was his trusted hands Oliver Wallace and Paul J. Smith), but for the songs he reached across the country to New York's renowned Tin Pan Alley, where he picked the songwriting team of Mack David, Jerry Livingston and Al Hoffman.

Walt met the trio while he was on a trip to New York. While there, he kept hearing on the radio a catchy novelty song, "Chi-Baba Chi-Baba," which the three had written and Perry Como had recorded. He was so taken with the song that he invited David, Livingston and Hoffman to audition for him.

"We played a medley of our songs for Walt, but you could see he liked 'Chi-Baba,'" said Livingston. "I think then he had in mind something similar for the fairy godmother's magic scene [in *Cinderella*]. But he didn't want something ordinary like 'Ali Kazam.'"

What he did get was **"Bibbidi-Bobbidi-Boo,"** a song in the same vein as "Chi-Baba" that proved so popular and so successful it was nominated for an Academy Award (the film's score was also nominated).

However, "Bibbidi-Bobbidi-Boo" wasn't the first song David, Livingston and Hoffman wrote for *Cinderella*. That honor went to **"A Dream Is a Wish Your Heart Makes."**

"When we went to play it for Walt, he simply said, 'That'll work,' and asked us to have a demo record made," recalled Livingston. "We weren't sure who to use for the vocal since we were new in Hollywood. Finally, Mack remembered that Ilene Woods, a singer we knew from the *Hit Parade*, was now living in Hollywood, so we used her. When Walt heard her voice, he got excited. The next thing we knew, she was hired for the voice of Cinderella."

The second milestone the film marked for Disney music was the establishment of the Studio's own music publishing company. This allowed Walt to finally control the rights to his songs and have whoever he liked record them.

The creation of the Walt Disney Music Company and Disneyland Records enabled the Disney Studios to release its own music, rather than rely on other companies. Shown here, a 1959 Disneyland record album and 1950 sheet music for Cinderella.

Jerry Livingston (seated), Mack David (middle) and Al Hoffman, the Disney "Tin Pan Alley" team, review songs for Cinderella.

23

The result was a parade of hit singles from the movie recorded by the likes of Perry Como and the Andrews Sisters. In fact, at one point in 1950, three songs from *Cinderella* were on the *Hit Parade*. "Bibbidi-Bobbidi-Boo" and "A Dream Is a Wish Your Heart Makes," both sung by Perry Como, shared the top two spots, while the Andrews Sisters' version of "The Work Song" was not far behind. The versions of "Bibbidi-Bobbidi-Boo" and "A Dream Is a Wish Your Heart Makes" heard in this collection are from the movie and feature vocals by Verna Felton as the Fairy Godmother and Ilene Woods as Cinderella, respectively.

In addition, the RCA album featuring songs from the film sold 750,000 copies in the first year, making it the number-one seller on *Billboard* magazine's pop album chart, a rare feat for what was considered a children's album.

For 1951's *Alice in Wonderland*, Walt went back to Tin Pan Alley, primarily because he felt the film would have an abundance of novelty songs, something the Tin Pan Alley gang was quite adept at producing. This time he turned to the songwriting team of Bob Hilliard and Sammy Fain, who contributed most of the tunes, including **"I'm Late."**

"The original version [of 'I'm Late'] was somewhat different, not as hur-

Alice falls down the rabbit hole in Alice in Wonderland. *Kathryn Beaumont (as Alice) is flanked by comedians Jerry Colonna (March Hare) and Ed Wynn (Mad Hatter) during a recording session for* Alice in Wonderland *(top right).*

ried," recalled Fain. "We had played it for Walt and he liked it. But that night I kept thinking about it and finally wrote out a second version. The next day I got in to see Walt and played it for him, and he was delighted. There are few studios I know of where you could get in to see the top man and have him change his mind on a song."

Perhaps the most famous and lasting song from *Alice in Wonderland* has been **"The Unbirthday Song,"** written by Mack David, Jerry Livingston and Al Hoffman, the team responsible for the songs in *Cinderella*. The tune comes during the Mad Hatter's tea party, which before the songwriting trio got hold of it, had proved to be one of the major sticking points in the film's development.

"One day Walt asked us to give it some thought, even though we weren't on the picture," said Livingston. "Here was a 10- to 15-minute major scene that they still didn't know quite how to handle. Finally, Mack David came up with the 'un-birthday' idea. Since there are 364 un-birthday days each year, it was a perfect reason for a mad tea party."

Alice in Wonderland features 14 original songs, more than any other Disney animated feature.

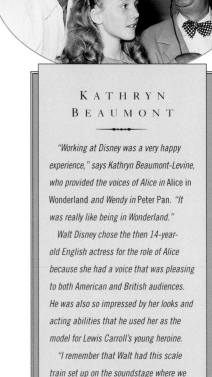

illiard and Fain wrote most of them. Seven other riters, including the David-Hoffman-Livingston am, also contributed songs.

Sammy Fain returned as the primary composer f songs for 1953's *Peter Pan*, but this time he orked with lyricist Sammy Cahn. Together the vo Sammys wrote five of the eight songs in the lm, including **"The Second Star to the Right"** nd **"You Can Fly! You Can Fly! You Can Fly!"**

Interestingly enough, Sammy Fain won an scar for Best Song for 1953, but it wasn't for anying he wrote for *Peter Pan*. He and lyricist Paul rancis Webster captured the award with "Secret ove" from the movie *Calamity Jane*. (A year ter it was Sammy Cahn's turn. He joined forces ith composer Jule Styne to take the Oscar for Three Coins in a Fountain" from the movie of e same name.)

When Walt Disney began work on 1955's *Lady nd the Tramp*, he chose singer Peggy Lee as the

voice for Lady. But as the story developed and Lee became more involved in the process, she began to see possibilities for songs throughout the movie. Walt was so impressed by her ideas and suggestions that he replaced her as Lady with Barbara Luddy — and gave her the task of writing all the songs for the film.

Lee did just that, teaming with Sonny Burke to write five tunes for *Lady and the Tramp*, including **"Bella Notte,"** which serves as the background music for the romantic spaghetti-eating scene involving Lady and Tramp. Lee's involvement wasn't limited to songwriting alone, though. She also provided the voices for Peg, Darling, the Siamese cats, and sang "He's a Tramp."

Aside from *Fantasia*, perhaps the most "adult" score written for a Disney animated feature was George Bruns' adaptation of Tchaikovsky's *Sleeping Beauty Ballet*, which as the score for the film *Sleeping Beauty* (1959) was nominated for an Academy Award.

Romance blooms for the canine stars of Lady and the Tramp *as Tony, the proprietor, sings "Bella Notte." (Above) The original 1955 sheet music by the Walt Disney Music Company.*

25

Peter Pan leads the Darling children to adventures in Never Land.

Bruns also co-wrote all of the songs for the film, except one — **"Once Upon a Dream,"** which was written by Sammy Fain and Jack Lawrence (with a giant nod to Tchaikovsky, upon whose music the song was based). Mary Costa as Briar Rose and Bill Shirley as Prince Phillip shared vocals for this most lovely of love songs.

Although none of the songs from *Sleeping Beauty* was nominated for an Academy Award, the Best Song selections looked like a *Who's Who* of composers who had at one time or another worked for Disney. The Oscar winner that year was "High Hopes," co-written by Sammy Cahn, who had contributed his talents to *Peter Pan*. Also nominated for 1959 were *Cinderella* and "The Unbirthday Song" writers Jerry Livingston and Mack David (for "The Hanging Tree"), "When You Wish Upon a Star" lyricist Ned Washington (for "Strange Are the Ways of Love") and Cahn again (for "The Best of Everything").

(Right) Sheet music published by Walt Disney Music Company, 1959.

"Cruella De Vil" is easily the most presumptuous song ever written for a Disney film. It's unknown whether its writer, Mel Leven, made quite the fortune off of it that the movie's Roger Radcliff did, but despite being a clever, catchy song, it didn't exactly burn up the pop charts in real life as it did in the make-believe world of 1961's *101 Dalmatians*.

Still, it has enjoyed something of a cult following, as evidenced by a 1988 version by the rock group the Replacements that proved to be an underground favorite on college and alternative radio stations.

GEORGE BRUNS

When George Bruns began working at the Disney Studio in 1955, one of his first assignments was to adapt Tchaikovsky's Sleeping Beauty Ballet *to the animated feature* Sleeping Beauty, *which was the next major production. That prompted the following anecdote involving Bruns and Walt Disney, as described by a Studio insider:*

George wrote some music for a sequence and Walt was called in to review it. The sequence was run and Walt said: "Looks good… and the music sounds great." Suddenly, someone realized that Walt hadn't met Bruns, so he said, "Oh, by the way Walt, this is George Bruns. He's doing the music for Sleeping Beauty."

George stood up to acknowledge the introduction — all 6'3" and 250 pounds of him! Walt looked at him in surprise and said, "I'm glad I didn't say anything bad about the music."

Bruns' score for Sleeping Beauty *was nominated for an Academy Award and signaled the beginning of his long and illustrious career with Disney. Bruns also scored such features as* 101 Dalmatians, The Absent-Minded Professor, Babes in Toyland, The Sword in the Stone, The Jungle Book *and* Robin Hood. *His songs include "Sleeping Beauty" from the movie of the same name, "The Workshop Song" from* Babes in Toyland *and "The Ballad of Davy Crockett" from the "Davy Crockett" series.*

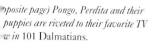

(Opposite page) Pongo, Perdita and their puppies are riveted to their favorite TV show in 101 Dalmatians.

(Left) Princess Aurora's forest friends gamely serve as dance partners in Sleeping Beauty. *(Right) Songwriter Roger Radcliff pens a popular tune in* 101 Dalmatians.

The Shermans' March Through Disney

Over the years, the Shermans have written over 200 songs for Disney films, television shows, theme parks and records, many of which have become timeless classics.

But then, it seemed only natural and fitting that the Shermans would end up working for Disney. "Our first impression of Hollywood when we arrived as youngsters in 1937 had been the street in front of the Carthay Circle Theater," recalled Robert Sherman. "It was resplendent with Disney characters from the premiere of *Snow White*. What a way to see Hollywood for the first time."

Walt was well acquainted with the brothers before he made them part of his staff. They'd

It seemed only natural that the Shermans would end up working for Disney...

n 1961 Walt Disney did something he'd never done before: he hired a couple of staff songwriters.

Walt had always employed staff composers, talented people such as Carl Stalling, Bert Lewis, Frank Churchill, Paul J. Smith, Oliver Wallace, Ed Plumb and George Bruns, to write and arrange the scores for his cartoons and features, but he'd never had anyone on staff whose sole job was to write songs. Whenever he needed a tune, he either turned to outside composers, such as Tin Pan Alley veterans and freelance songwriters Sammy Fain and Sammy Cahn, or he gave the assignment to his staff composers, who, although exceedingly proficient at the melodies, inevitably turned to anyone they could at the Studio for the words (as was the case with the songs in *Snow White and the Seven Dwarfs*, which featured music by Churchill and lyrics by Larry Morey, whose "day" job was as a sequence director for the film).

But in 1961 Walt hired a couple of songwriting brothers by the names of Richard M. and Robert B. Sherman. It turned out to be a good move.

composed music for the *Zorro* television series as freelance writers and, more significantly, had written several songs for Annette Funicello, including the pop hits "Tall Paul" and "Jo-Jo the Dog-Faced Boy," which she'd recorded on Disneyland Records. (In all, the Shermans wrote 36 songs for Annette, including **"Strummin' Song"** and **"Mister Piano Man."**)

Songwriters Richard Sherman (left) and Robert Sherman (right) review the music for Mary Poppins *with the film's co-producer and writer, Bill Walsh (center).*

THE SHERMAN BROTHERS

Prior to joining Disney, Richard and Robert Sherman wrote songs for Annette Funicello, which brought them to the attention of Walt Disney.

"Walt needed a song for this picture starring Annette," recalls Richard. ' "Who are those guys who write rock and roll songs? Bring them in here to do this song." '

So the Shermans wrote "Strummin' Song" for The Horsemasters, *a two-part drama scheduled to air on "Walt Disney's Wonderful World of Color" in 1961. But that's not the end of the story.*

The two brothers showed up in Disney's office one day to play the song for him. "But he started telling us about an entirely different picture," says Robert, "about these two girls who meet at summer camp and they're twins."

Even after they were able to play "Strummin' Song" for him, Disney could not get his mind off the other movie. So he handed the Shermans a script and told them to take a crack at the title song.

At that time, the movie was called "We Belong Together." So the brothers wrote a catchy pop song called "Let's Get Together."

Disney liked it, but there was one problem: the title of the movie had changed. So the Shermans wrote another song, "For Now, for Always." Disney liked that song, too, only there was still another problem. The title of the movie had changed again.

By the time Disney finally settled upon "The Parent Trap" as the title for the movie, the Sherman brothers had written four songs in four completely different styles. Fortunately, their work did not go for naught. All of the songs ended up in the movie, including the final title tune, "The Parent Trap" (sung, by the way, by Tommy Sands and Annette).

(Left) Former Mouseketeer Annette Funicello starring in The Golden Horseshoe Revue, *a 1962 musical variety show originally featured on "Walt Disney's Wonderful World of Color" and later released theatrically.*

Young Wart, the boy who would be King Arthur, approaches his destiny in The Sword in the Stone.

As Richard Sherman recalled, "We really fell in love with the stories. When we next met with Walt, we showed him the seven stories we selected as our choices for the film. He reached

"We wanted to do a full-blown musical fantasy…"

over and got his copy of the book, and we discovered we had picked the same seven chapters that he had already decided to use in the film."

The Shermans began working with screenwriter Don DaGradi on a story treatment while at the same time roughing out a few songs.

"From the very beginning, we saw this in musical terms," said Richard Sherman. "We wanted to do a full-blown musical fantasy of the first magnitude. To achieve this, we set the story back in time to Edwardian London. We were able to convince Walt that this was the way to proceed. It also gave us the chance to write music and lyrics with an English 'folk' and 'music hall' flavor."

The first animated feature the Shermans worked on was *The Sword in the Stone* (1963), to which they contributed six songs, including "**Higitus Figitus**," a nonsense song in the "Bibbidi-Bobbidi-Boo" vein.

The film was the Shermans' first real test at writing songs for an entire film. Up to that point, their talents had been used primarily to write isolated songs for such Disney live-action pictures as *Moon Pilot*, *Bon Voyage* and *Son of Flubber*.

Apparently Walt was pleased with their efforts on *The Sword in the Stone* because one of their next assignments was to write the songs for the movie that would become the crowning achievement of his long career: *Mary Poppins*.

The Shermans became involved in the project in 1960 when Walt gave them a series of short stories by P.L. Travers built around a magical English nanny.

But there was one hitch to all these grand plans. Walt couldn't get the rights to the stories, though he'd been trying for close to 20 years. Travers simply refused to sell them because she felt no one could do justice to her stories or her characters.

Finally, in 1962, with the help of DaGradi's story outline and several songs the Shermans had written, Walt was able to persuade Travers to sell him the rights to *Mary Poppins*. It was full speed ahead.

"Writing songs for *Mary Poppins* was a songwriter's dream," said Robert Sherman. "Each song we did had a purpose, a reason for being."

One of the first the pair wrote for the movie (written before Walt had secured the rights to the stories) was **"Supercalifragilisticexpialidocious,"** a tune inspired by a childhood experience of the Shermans.

"When we were little boys in summer camp in the Adirondack Mountains in the mid-1930s," explained Richard Sherman, "we heard this word. Not the exact word, but a word very similar to 'supercal.' It was a word that was longer than 'antidisestablishmentarianism,' and it gave us kids a word that no adult had. It was our own special word, and we wanted the Banks children to have that same feeling."

Richard Sherman (at piano) fine tunes the songs for Mary Poppins *with (from left) Robert Sherman, arranger/conductor Irwin Kostal, Dick Van Dyke and Julie Andrews.*

Actress Julie Andrews, who played Mary Poppins (and won an Academy Award for her performance) contributed to the creation of another tune in the film. "We needed a song early in the film that would establish a theme for Mary Poppins." said Richard. "At first, we came up with a syrupy ballad. But when Julie heard it, she asked that we do something with more bounce to it."

The result was a **"A Spoonful of Sugar,"** the song Mary Poppins sings to get the Banks children to clean their room. The melody line for the tune also became the leitmotif the film's musical arranger Irwin Kostal subtly uses to herald the appearance of Mary Poppins in scenes throughout the movie.

One song the Shermans struggled with was a theme song for the chimney sweep, Bert, played by Dick Van Dyke. "One day Bob [Sherman] came up with a line 'One chimney, two chimney, three chimney sweep,'" said Richard Sherman. "I left the room, the words running through my head, when suddenly I heard a melody line in my head that fit the words. I rushed back to Bob and played it on the piano. That was the birth of **'Chim Chim Cher-ee.'"**

"Supercalifragilisticexpialidocious"

(Opposite page) Dick Van Dyke, Karen Dotrice, Matthew Garber and Julie Andrews in Mary Poppins. *(Left) Richard Sherman, Julie Andrews and Robert Sherman share a happy moment after winning Academy Awards for their work in* Mary Poppins.

DICK VAN DYKE

On the screen, Mary Poppins seemed to be the most British of movies. The setting, the story, the cast, all were British, except for one very important exception. For the character of Bert the chimney sweep, Walt Disney chose American actor Dick Van Dyke.

"I really don't know why," says Van Dyke, "but I'm glad he did. Making that movie was one of the greatest experiences I've had. I knew from the moment I read the script and heard the songs it was going to be a classic."

Van Dyke surmises that Disney knew about him from his work in the Broadway and Hollywood versions of Bye Bye Birdie and his successful television series, "The Dick Van Dyke Show." But that still doesn't explain why an American actor would get the role of a British chimney sweep.

"I never even had to do a screen test," says Van Dyke. "I guess Walt was just convinced that I was the right one for the part."

However, garnering the part of the old banker in the movie wasn't as easy. "Walt made me make a contribution to his art school [California Institute of the Arts] before he'd give me that role," says Van Dyke.

In all, 14 songs written by the Sherman brothers are featured in *Mary Poppins*. Their effort paid off handsomely. Their Music earned the Shermans an Oscar for Best Original Music Score while "Chim Chim Cher-ee" brought them another for Best Song. In addition, "Supercalifragilisticexpialidocious" became a pop hit, entering the *Billboard* Hot 100 in August, 1965.

The music wasn't the only successful aspect of *Mary Poppins*, however. The film itself was a critical and commercial hit, garnering 13 Academy Award nominations, including Best Picture. All told, the movie won five Academy Awards.

Meanwhile, back at the Studio, the Sherman brothers were writing more songs for more Disney projects.

During the filming of *Mary Poppins*, they were asked to come up with a song for a short feature based on A.A. Milne's *Winnie the Pooh* stories. Although the two brothers enjoyed reading the tales, they just couldn't seem to come up with anything that truly caught the spirit of the lovable English bear.

Then one day they sat down with the costume designer for *Mary Poppins*, Englishman Tony Walton (who was then married to Julie Andrews).

"Since he was raised in England, we thought he might have some insights," said Richard Sherman. They were right. Walton spent two full hours talking about *Winnie the Pooh*, enthusiastically explaining how important the Milne stories were to him while he was growing up.

"It was like a door opening up," said Richard. "All of a sudden we understood how to read the stories, and we reread them and got this kind of joyous abandon. We could go into that hundred acre wood and be those characters… and then the songs just started flowing out of us. It was delightful."

The result was **"Winnie the Pooh,"** which is heard in the three Pooh featurettes, *Winnie the Pooh and the Honey Tree* (1966), *Winnie the Pooh and the Blustery Day* (which won the Oscar for Best Cartoon Short Subject in 1968) and *Winnie the Pooh and Tigger, Too* (1974).

The next animated feature the Sherman brothers worked on was *The Jungle Book* (1967), but by the time they became involved the film was already well into development. In fact, one key song had already been written for the movie.

Young Mowgli takes a break with Baloo in The Jungle Book.

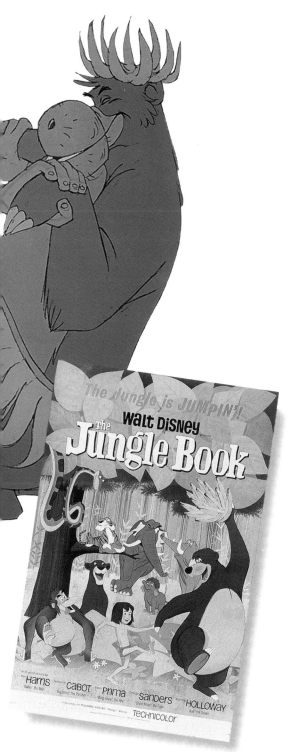

"It's quite a good song," Walt Disney told them, "but it [the picture] needs a whole bunch of new songs, and they've got to be fun songs."

The Shermans ended up writing five of the six tunes for *The Jungle Book*, including **"I Wan'na Be Like You,"** a free-wheeling scat song sung in the movie by King Louie, who was voiced by the King of Scat himself, Louis Prima.

By the way, the one song in the film not written by the Shermans (the "quite" good one) is **"The Bare Necessities,"** penned by Terry Gilkyson and performed by Phil Harris as Baloo the Bear. The song proved good enough to earn an Academy Award nomination.

By now, you must have the feeling that the Sherman brothers have played a fairly large and important role in the Disney musical legacy and you're right. But we're not done yet. And neither were the Shermans.

For the 1970 animated feature *The Aristocats*, the Sherman brothers contributed three more songs, including the title tune, sung by Maurice Chevalier.

The fact that Chevalier even agreed to sing **"The Aristocats"** was something of a surprise.

The voice of Scatman Crothers jazzes up the vocals in The Aristocats.

MAURICE CHEVALIER AND THE SHERMANS

The relationship between Maurice Chevalier and the Sherman family goes all the way back. In the 1930 film, The Big Pond, *with Claudette Colbert, Chevalier sang "Livin' in the Sunlight, Lovin' in the Moonlight," written by Al Sherman.*

In 1962's In Search of the Castaways *with Hayley Mills, Chevalier sang "Enjoy It," a song written by Al Sherman's sons Richard and Robert.*

"Walt knew about the connection," says Robert Sherman, "so he set up a reunion at the Studio. He invited our mom, our dad and Maurice, and we had lunch together. It was a beautiful thing."

In addition to working with Chevalier on Monkeys, Go Home! *and* The Aristocats, *the Sherman brothers also unwittingly provided the French crooner with two songs for his next album.*

"While he was here in the States making Monkeys, Go Home!," *says Richard, "he went to Disneyland and saw* It's a Small World *and* Carousel of Progress… *He didn't know we'd written the songs for them. He said, 'I love those songs. I want to record them.' So in his next album, he recorded them, plus 'Joie de Vivre' [from* Monkeys, Go Home!*]."*

"Not only that," adds Robert, "for the last two or three years of his life, he opened his shows with 'It's a Small World' and closed them with 'There's a Great Big Beautiful Tomorrow.' We were very honored by that."

33

Robert Sherman (left) and Richard Sherman (far right) join Angela Lansbury and David Tomlinson during the filming of Bedknobs and Broomsticks.

"The songs you write for a production are not necessarily meant to be hit songs. They're meant to work for a scene, they're meant to work for a situation or character."

Richard Sherman

The French crooner had retired a few years earlier at the age of 80, but Walt Disney himself had already talked Chevalier into making a comeback once, for *Monkeys, Go Home!* (1967).

Chevalier later wrote of his agreeing to record "The Aristocats": "I would not have done it for anybody else and for any kind of money, except the honour of showing my love and admiration for the one and only Walt."

Ironically, Chevalier's singing of the song was a posthumous tribute to Walt Disney, who died December 15, 1966, several months before the release of *The Jungle Book* and before *The Aristocats* was even put into production. It just shows the respect people had for him that his influence lived on long after he had passed on.

Another song in *The Aristocats*, **"Ev'rybody Wants to Be a Cat,"** was written by Floyd Huddleston and Al Rinker with Louis Armstrong in mind. But when the jazz trumpeter was unable to take the role of Scat Cat, Scatman Crothers took over. The song also features vocals by Phil Harris, among others.

The last movie the Sherman brothers worked on as staff songwriters for the Disney Studio was *Bedknobs and Broomsticks*, the 1971 fantasy picture that, like *Mary Poppins*, was based on an English story, this one by Mary Norton.

Walt actually acquired the rights to *Bedknobs and Broomsticks* first and at one point became so exasperated over the negotiations with P.L. Travers for *Mary Poppins* that he considered going ahead with *Bedknobs and Broomsticks*.

"I remember that just before everything got going on *Poppins*, we were having some trouble getting okays from P.L. Travers on the songs we had written for it," recalled Robert Sherman. "One day Walt came to us and said, 'Don't worry, boys, I've bought us another story that deals with magic. If we can't work things out with Travers, we'll be able to use your stuff in the other picture.'"

"Supercalifragilisticexpialidocious" in *Bedknobs and Broomsticks*? Of course, that didn't happen. Instead, years later, when the movie finally was made, the Shermans wrote a whole new batch of tunes, including **"The Age of Not Believing,"** sung by Angela Lansbury. Both the song and the song score were nominated for Oscars.

Another tune the Sherman brothers wrote for *Bedknobs and Broomsticks*, **"Nobody's Problems,"** was also sung by Lansbury, but it was cut from the final version of the film.

THE BRINY BOYS

The Age Of Not Believing

Music and Lyrics by RICHARD M. SHERMAN *and* ROBERT B. SHERMAN

WALT DISNEY PRODUCTIONS PRESENTS

Bedknobs and Broomsticks

FROM WALT DISNEY PRODUCTIONS MOTION PICTURE "BEDKNOBS and BROOMSTICKS"

Angela LANSBURY David TOMLINSON

TECHNICOLOR

WONDERLAND MUSIC CO., INC.
WALT DISNEY PRODUCTIONS LTD.

Beginning in the 1970s, the Disney Studio went back to bringing in outside writers whenever a song was needed for a film.

In 1973, it was "King of the Road's" Roger Miller, who wrote and sang two ballads for *Robin Hood*, one of which is **"Oo-De-Lally,"** an ode to Robin Hood's favorite expression.

In 1977, it was Sammy Fain, returning to the Studio for the first time since writing songs for *Alice in Wonderland*, *Peter Pan* and *Sleeping Beauty*, and recent Oscar-winning songwriters Al Kasha and Joel Hirschhorn.

Teaming with lyricists Carol Connors and Ayn Robbins (who also wrote the other three songs in the movie), Fain (an Oscar-winner himself, though not for any of his work for Disney) penned **"Someone's Waiting for You"** for *The Rescuers*.

Hirschhorn and Kasha, who won Academy Awards for "Morning After" from *The Poseidon Adventure* (1972) and "We May Never Love Like This Again" from *The Towering Inferno* (1974), wrote the songs for *Pete's Dragon* (1977), a film combining live action

(Above left) Allan-a-Dale, the troubadour rooster, croons Country and Western thanks to Roger Miller. (Above) Terry-Thomas records the slithery voice of Sir Hiss for Robin Hood.

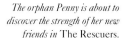

35

The orphan Penny is about to discover the strength of her new friends in The Rescuers.

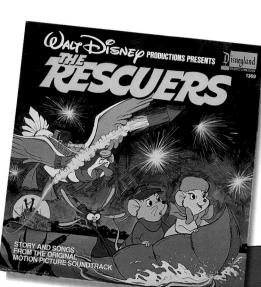

and animation that was based on a 13-page story synopsis Walt had approved before his death. One of the songs the duo wrote was **"Candle on the Water,"** sung by Helen Reddy in the movie.

Both "Someone's Waiting for You" and "Candle on the Water" were nominated for Academy Awards (along with "The Slipper and the Rose Waltz" written by Richard and Robert Sherman, who were now writing for other studios).

In 1981, songwriters Stan Fidel and Richard Johnston were brought in to write a song for *The Fox and the Hound* and they came up with **"Best of Friends,"** which featured Pearl Bailey on vocals.

And in 1988, Barry Manilow joined with lyricists Jack Feldman and Bruce Sussman (of "Copacabana" fame), to write **"Perfect Isn't Easy"** for *Oliver & Company*. The song features vocals by Bette Midler (as the character of Georgette, a spoiled, pampered poodle) and was something of a reunion for Midler and Manilow (Manilow had been Midler's arranger and accompanist early in her career).

"Best of Friends" captures the sentiments of young companions in The Fox and the Hound.

CANDLE ON THE WATER

Words and Music by
AL KASHA and JOEL HIRSCHHORN

from Walt Disney Productions'
PETE'S DRAGON

(Left) Pete and his towering green friend Elliott in a scene from Pete's Dragon.

Oliver & Company represented a modest yet significant step for Disney animated films: a return to the full-scale musical features for which the Studio had become known throughout the years, but which had become increasingly rare in recent decades.

The movie featured five tunes, all adhering to an old Disney maxim: the songs should play an integral and prominent part in the story without overshadowing or disrupting it.

"Music should come out of the dialogue," said the film's director, George Scribner, reemphasizing a point Walt Disney had made many times many years before. "The best music advances the story or defines a character. The challenge was to figure out areas in our film where music could better express a concept or idea."

Perhaps no one knew this better than a New York-based lyricist named Howard Ashman, who with Barry Mann wrote **"Once Upon a Time in New York City,"** performed by Huey Lewis over the opening credits of *Oliver & Company*.

When Ashman was approached about working on the next Disney animated feature, *The Little Mermaid* (1989), he jumped at the chance.

"Animation is the last great place to do Broadway musicals," said Ashman, who wrote the off-Broadway sensation *Little Shop of Horrors* with his writing partner, Alan Menken. "It's a place you can use a whole other set of skills and a way of working which is more the way plays and musicals are made. With most films, the story seems to come first and the songs are an afterthought."

"Coming from a musical theater background," he continued, "Alan and I are used to writing songs for characters in situations. For *The Little Mermaid* we wanted songs that would really move the story forward and keep things driving ahead."

To do this, both writers felt it was important for them to be involved in the project from the start. If this sounds familiar, there's a good reason. In the Disney Studio's early days, staff musicians routinely worked with the animation team during the formative stages of an animated feature and the results were such films as *Snow White and the Seven Dwarfs*, *Pinocchio* and *Bambi*.

"Animation is the last great place to do Broadway musicals."

(Left) Oliver meets a motley crew in Oliver & Company. *(Right) Ariel and friends in* The Little Mermaid.

Calypso underwater — a full scale musical delight in The Little Mermaid.

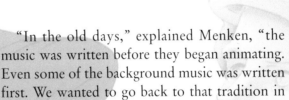

"In the old days," explained Menken, "the music was written before they began animating. Even some of the background music was written first. We wanted to go back to that tradition in *The Little Mermaid* by laying the songs out early in the story development process."

What Ashman and Menken wanted to achieve with *The Little Mermaid* was nothing less than the classic style of those early Disney animated features. The success of the film, both critically and commercially, seems to indicate that they reached their goal. Not only did *The Little Mermaid* break all box office records for an animated feature, it won Academy Awards for Best Song and Best Original Score.

The seven songs heard in the movie took Ashman and Menken 18 months to write and fine tune.

"Writing the songs is usually pretty easy," said Ashman. "The hard part is what we call 'routining,' which means deciding how many times to repeat a part, if at all, or whether to cut it out entirely."

"Part of Your World," sung by Jodi Benson as the voice of Ariel, is used to introduce the character and articulate her dreams.

"In almost every musical ever written," said Ashman, "there's a place, usually early in the show, where the leading

The movie broke the box office records set by *Mermaid* and the songs written by the duo were inundated by awards, including Oscars for Best Song and Best Original Score, and plaudits, such as this one from *Newsweek* magazine: "The most delicious musical score of 1991 is Alan Menken and Howard Ashman's *Beauty and the Beast*. If the growing armada of titanically troubled Broadway musicals had half its charm and affectionate cleverness, the ships wouldn't be foundering."

Before Ashman and then Menken became involved in the film in 1989, *Beauty and the Beast* was a serious drama with little music and no humor. According to producer Don Hahn, Ashman was the person who convinced the creative team to steer the film in another direction.

"He came up with the idea of turning the enchanted objects into living creatures with unique personalities," said Hahn. "That was a big breakthrough. He was also the driving creative force in terms of musicalizing the script."

With Ashman and Menken aboard, production on *Beauty and the Beast* began in late 1989.

"One of the first things Howard and I did when we began working on this project was to sit down and toss around some musical ideas," said Menken. "He usually had a basic idea of the style of song he wanted to write and sometimes even a title or some completed lyrics. Then he would ask what the music might sound like if we were going to write a certain kind of song and I would sit at the piano and let fly. Howard had the ability

lady... sings about what she wants most out of life. We borrowed this classic rule of Broadway musical construction for 'Part of Your World.'"

Of course, such a scene was nothing new to Disney animated features— *Snow White*, *Cinderella* and *Sleeping Beauty* had done the same thing long before Ariel— it's just that no Disney heroine had done it in 30 years.

For the character of Sebastian (voiced by Samuel E. Wright), who sings the Academy Award-nominated **"Kiss the Girl"** and the Academy Award-*winning* **"Under the Sea,"** Ashman and Menken introduced a Caribbean flavor to the music that allowed for both a rhythmic edge and a contemporary feel.

"We came up with the idea of giving Sebastian a Caribbean flavor," said Ashman, "so that we could have a whole range of calypso and reggae styles to play with in the music. It was a way of adding energy, spice and a little bit of contemporary pop feeling."

For an encore, Ashman and Menken wrote the songs and music for *Beauty and the Beast* (1991) and, by all accounts, they managed to surpass the success they enjoyed with *The Little Mermaid*.

"We wanted to go back to that tradition... laying out the songs early in the story development process."

Alan Menken

Lumiere and Mrs. Potts lend advice to the Beast (top), while Belle resists Gaston's advances in Beauty and the Beast.

to find what he liked and then write to it. We had a kind of shorthand between us and we each shared a background of loving musicals and growing up with many of the same influences."

The two wrote six songs for the film, including the Academy Award-nominated **"Be Our Guest"** and the Academy Award-winning **"Beauty and the Beast."** (A third song, "Belle," was also nominated, making *Beauty and the Beast* the first motion picture ever to have three songs from the same film nominated for an Academy Award. The film was also the first animated feature to be nominated for Best Picture.)

"Be Our Guest" was originally intended to be sung to Belle's father Maurice. "The song had already been recorded and the sequence partially

"In all of our projects, we had never achieved the liftable ballad..."

animated when we decided that it would be more meaningful if it was directed towards Belle," said Gary Trousdale, one of the film's directors. "After all, she is one of the two main characters and the story revolves around her coming to the castle. We had to bring all the vocal talents back into the studio to change all references to gender that appeared in the original recording."

According to Menken, simplicity is the key to the song "Beauty and the Beast." "We wanted it to be gentler and smaller, as opposed to some ballads that are large and heroic in scope. The song was written with Angela Lansbury in mind and we kept imagining her voice and what a fine actor she is, as well as a singer."

Menken also admitted he and Ashman had an ulterior motive. "In all our projects, we had never achieved the liftable ballad," he told *Newsweek*. "We were determined to have it this time."

They got it. In addition to Lansbury's rendition in the movie (and in this collection), a pop version of the song was recorded by Celine Dion and Peabo Bryson (it's heard over the closing credits and, yes, it became a hit, reaching the Top 10 on the *Billboard* magazine Hot 100 chart).

The songwriting team of Howard Ashman (left) and Alan Menken received Academy Awards for their work on The Little Mermaid *and* Beauty and the Beast.

Disney's Live-Action Musical Legacy

Walt Disney's expansion into live-action movies was slow and gradual. He used live action in *The Reluctant Dragon* (1941) as a way to string together unrelated cartoon segments. He also used it in such movies as *Saludos Amigos*, *The Three Caballeros*, *Song of the South* and *So Dear to My Heart*, but he couldn't quite make the leap away from making a film without any animation.

(*So Dear to My Heart* is a good example: the movie was supposed to be entirely live action, but Walt's distributor at the time, RKO, felt a Disney film would not sell unless it had at least some animation in it. So Walt reluctantly

Disney approached the process of live-action movie making differently than other studios.

added several minor cartoon sequences. The consensus among film critics is that the animation segments keep the movie from being any better than it is because they seem to intrude unnecessarily on the live action.)

In 1949, with a war-ravaged England freezing payments due to American film companies, the Disney Studio decided to use the money it had made there (money that could only be spent in England) to begin producing live-action motion pictures in the United Kingdom.

The first to be made was *Treasure Island* (1950), based on Robert Louis Stevenson's classic novel. Walt spent a couple of weeks in England watching the filming, and upon his return told his animators how much fun he'd had and how much easier it was to do live action than animation. The animators saw the writing on the wall. Said one, "We realized that as soon as Walt rode on a camera crane, we were going to lose him."

Naturally that wasn't true. He didn't abandon his animators or animation (*Cinderella*, *Alice in Wonderland* and *Peter Pan* are testament to that). But he was taken with the idea of getting into the live-action movie business. After all, he could make them faster and cheaper than animated features and, more importantly, he could make more of them (several a year, as opposed to animated films, which took several years).

The ultimate boy-and-his-dog story, Old Yeller *stars Kevin Corcoran. The lyrics to the title song were penned by Gil George, the Studio's nurse.*

(Upper left) Bach's "Toccata and Fugue in D Minor," which was featured in Fantasia, *is reprised in an eerie new light by Captain Nemo in* 20,000 Leagues Under the Sea. *(Lower left) Captain Nemo battles a giant squid atop his submarine.*

(Above) Darby O'Gill and the Little People *features a rare musical performance by Sean Connery.*

the Sea (1954). The song was written by Norman Gimbel and Al Hoffman (the same Hoffman who, with Jerry Livingston and Mack David, had written songs for *Cinderella* and *Alice in Wonderland*).

Before he hired the Sherman brothers as staff songwriters in 1961, Walt Disney had two options when it came to writing songs for his movies. He could either hire outside songwriters or he could turn to his music department, which wasn't a problem when he just needed scores or melodies, but words were another problem. His music staff was made up of composers, not lyricists. So, for the words, the staff composers usually turned to anyone who was ready, willing and able, be they animator, scriptwriter, story editor or, in the case of **"Old Yeller,"** the Studio nurse.

However, Walt approached the process of live-action movie making differently than other studios, applying knowledge and principles he'd learned from his years in animation to the production of the live-action pictures.

One example was his use of storyboarding, which involves laying out the entire movie using hand-drawn scenes that are placed on boards so that the sequence of action or events can be planned prior to shooting any film.

Another was the use of songs. Not only did Walt believe they should be a part of his live-action movies, he also felt they should be used the same way as in his animated features. That is, they should be an integral part of the story, moving it forward without bogging it down.

One of the first songs to appear in a Disney live-action movie was a little sea chantey sung by the unlikeliest of singers. When one thinks of Kirk Douglas, "singer" doesn't immediately come to mind, but there's Douglas crooning **"A Whale of a Tale"** in *20,000 Leagues Under*

(Right) Ed Wynn, Annette Funicello, Tommy Sands and Kevin Corcoran in *Babes in Toyland.*

HAYLEY MILLS

While Walt Disney was casting Swiss Family Robinson, *he viewed a movie called* Tiger Bay *starring well-known British actor John Mills, whom he was considering for the role of the father. But while watching* Tiger Bay *he was struck by the performance of a young actress who just happened to be Mills's daughter.*

Wasting no time, Disney immediately signed 13-year-old Hayley Mills to a contract, and a year later she made her Disney debut in Pollyanna.

Over the next five years, Mills played twin sisters in The Parent Trap, *sang a duet with Maurice Chevalier while stranded in a tree in* In Search of the Castaways, *crooned with Burl Ives in* Summer Magic, *got mixed up in international intrigue in* The Moon-Spinners *and owned a pretty smart feline in* That Darn Cat.

As for her father, he ended up getting the role in Swiss Family Robinson. *Perhaps Hayley put in a good word for him.*

For *Old Yeller* (1957), Disney music director Oliver Wallace turned to Gil George to help him write the title song, performed by Jerome Courtland over the opening credits. George in reality was Disney Studio nurse Hazel George, who proved such a handy musical wordsmith that she also provided the lyrics for songs in the Disney movies *Westward Ho the Wagons!*, *Perri* and *Tonka*.

Darby O'Gill and the Little People (1959) features **"Pretty Irish Girl,"** a short ditty written by Wallace and Larry Watkin (who earlier had written the screenplay for *Treasure Island*).

Okay, so what makes it so special? Well, "Pretty Irish Girl" is sung by a young Scottish

(Left) Hayley Mills, Maureen O'Hara, Brian Keith, and Hayley Mills in The Parent Trap, *a film that gave Mills her first and only hit song.*

actor who, although unknown at that time, would later gain a little more notoriety playing a character who goes by the name of Bond… James Bond. That's right, this is your chance to hear Sean Connery sing. Featured here is an original demo version, never-before-released.

In 1961 the Disney Studio released its first live-action musical, *Babes in Toyland*, which was based on Victor Herbert's classic 1903 operetta and included new music by Disney staff composer George Bruns (whose work was nominated for an Academy Award).

The film starred teen heartthrobs Annette Funicello and Tommy Sands as the storybook sweethearts Mary Contrary and Tom Piper, but it was the villainous Barnaby, played by Ray Bolger (of the Scarecrow in *Wizard of Oz* fame), who stole the show, especially with his rendition of Herbert's **"Castle in Spain."**

Although the first film songs Richard and Robert Sherman wrote for Disney were for 1961's *The Parent Trap* (including **"The Parent Trap"**), the first effort of theirs to actually appear in a Disney movie was some lyrics they wrote to the tune "Sweet Betsy of Pike." The newly remodeled song became the "Medfield Fight Song" for *The Absent-Minded Professor* (1961).

Thereafter, their assignments became increasingly meatier and included the song scores for such features as *The Sword in the Stone*, *Mary Poppins* and *Bedknobs and Broomsticks*.

One of their first efforts at writing a musical came in 1962 when they wrote the song score for

(Above) Summer Magic, *starring Burl Ives, Hayley Mills and Dorothy McGuire, introduced seven new songs by the Sherman brothers.*

Special effects created amazing moments in Darby O'Gill and the Little People.

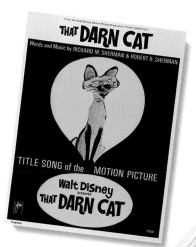

In Search of the Castaways. The movie featured four tunes, including **"Enjoy It,"** which found Maurice Chevalier and Hayley Mills performing while stranded in a tree.

Their next musical, *Summer Magic* (1963), was even more ambitious. Featuring seven songs, including **"On the Front Porch,"** the movie served as something of a dress rehearsal for *Mary Poppins,* which would come a year later. "On the Front Porch" is performed by the venerable Burl Ives, who had last sung for Disney in *So Dear to My Heart.*

Perhaps the most interesting song the Shermans wrote for Disney, in terms of who performed it, was **"The Monkey's Uncle"** from the 1965 movie of the same name. The film itself is a lighthearted youth comedy starring Tommy Kirk and Annette Funicello. The song, written with a popular surf beat, features Annette Funicello on lead vocals and the Beach Boys on soaring backing harmonies.

The Shermans created a jazz-flavored title tune in the style of "Mack the Knife" for the 1965 film *That Darn Cat.* Although Bobby Darin sings the title song in the film, it was this version by actor-songwriter Bobby Troup that was featured on the Disney album release and made it onto the pop charts. Troup may be better known as the writer of the 1964 hit "(Get Your Kicks on) Route 66," as well as his starring role in the 1970s television series *Emergency!*

In 1966, flush with confidence over the success of *Mary Poppins* (and the popularity of such other grand musicals as *My Fair Lady* and *The Sound of Music*), Walt Disney put the Sherman brothers to work on a big-budget, live-action musical he had planned called *The Happiest Millionaire* (1967).

The movie was based on a 1956 Broadway play of the same name, but the stage show had not been a musical. Enter the Shermans. They penned 12 songs for *The Happiest Millionaire,* including **"Fortuosity,"** performed by Broadway star Tommy Steele, who was upstaged during the number's reprise by a live alligator.

45

"Walt knew his people and their potentials better than they knew themselves. Most importantly, Walt gave each of his pictures heart, that indefinable quality that ultimately touches our emotions."

Richard and Robert Sherman

TV Tunes

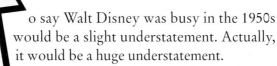

To say Walt Disney was busy in the 1950s would be a slight understatement. Actually, it would be a huge understatement.

Not only did Walt expand from animated features into live-action pictures, he also began producing television shows and series and built Disneyland. And in true Disney fashion, music played a large role in each.

"This was a hectic time at the Studio," recalled Buddy Baker, who joined the Disney music staff following a career in big bands and radio, "We had the weekly series ["Disneyland," which later became "The Wonderful World of Disney," among other titles] to write music for, plus the daily show ["The Mickey Mouse Club"]. This was in addition to the feature films the Studio was producing. And Walt demanded quality, whether it was music for a multi million-dollar animated feature or a television show."

By all accounts, Walt got the quality he wanted. In fact, he got more than that. Many of the songs written during this time, especially those written for his TV shows, became not only hit tunes, but bona fide Disney classics that are as recognizable and warmly regarded today as they were 40 years ago when they were first introduced.

October 3, 1955. 5 p.m. A popular and famous spelling cadence is heard on the ABC television network for the very first time: M - I - C - K - E - Y   M - O - U - S - E. The "Mickey Mouse Club," one of the most popular children's television shows ever, debuts on ABC, starring Annette, Cubby, Darlene and the rest of the Mouseketeers, as well as one of the best-known and best-loved songs of all time, the **"Mickey Mouse Club March,"** written by the Club's adult host, Jimmie Dodd.

Dodd also wrote the **"Mickey Mouse Club Alma Mater"** ("Why? Because we like you!"), as well as the theme songs for two educational series that were introduced in 1956 as part of the "Mickey Mouse Club." **"I'm No Fool"** kicked off six animated shorts about safety (the particular song featured in this collection is from "I'm No Fool with a Bicycle") and **"You, the Human Animal,"** which was heard in the series of the same name. Both were sung by Cliff Edwards reprising his role as the conscience conscious Jiminy Cricket.

Walt Disney's first weekly prime time show on television was "Disneyland," an anthology series that debuted on ABC in 1954. The show

47

(Opposite) Members of the "Mickey Mouse Club" in a group shot with Walt Disney.
(Left) Cliff Edwards, the seldom seen face behind the voice of Jiminy Cricket.

After the premiere of "Walt Disney's Wonderful World of Color" in 1961, sales of color televisions skyrocketed.

"The Ballad of Davy Crockett" became the fastest-selling record in 1955.

was hosted by Walt himself, and each week featured cartoons or feature films from the Disney library, original shows and behind-the-scenes glimpses of Disneyland, which was then under construction.

The series, with various changes in names and networks, remained on the air for 26 years. One of those changes was in 1961 when the show moved to NBC and was renamed "Walt Disney's Wonderful World of Color,"— and for good reason: The show was now being broadcast in color (a boon to television manufacturers and salespeople, who saw sales of color TVs skyrocket). Along with the new network, the new name and the new color format, Walt had the ubiquitous Sherman brothers write a new theme song called, cleverly enough, **"Wonderful World of Color (Main Title)."**

The premiere episode of "Walt Disney's Wonderful World of Color," broadcast September 24, 1961, was "An Adventure in Color," starring a brand-new Disney animated character, Ludwig Von Drake. The show, which was ostensibly about the wonders of color, featured Von Drake

singing **"The Spectrum Song,"** written by the Sherman brothers, of course. The song is a clever play on words and colors and, if you pay particularly close attention to the end, you'll hear a reference to an earlier Disney song.

Before the motion pictures *Davy Crockett, King of the Wild Frontier* (1955) and *Davy Crockett and the River Pirates* (1956), there was "Davy Crockett," the television series. In fact, those two movies *were* the television series (the Davy Crockett stories proved so popular on the "Disneyland" television show that Walt decided to edit them together and release them as movies).

But even before there was a "Davy Crockett" television series, there was **"The Ballad of Davy Crockett."**

"Walt needed what I call a little 'throwaway' tune that would bridge the time gaps in the story of Davy Crockett," recalled staff composer George Bruns (of *Sleeping Beauty* fame). "He needed a song that would carry the story from one sequence to another. I threw together the melody line and chorus, 'Davy, Davy Crockett, King of the Wild Frontier,' in about 30 minutes."

Tom Blackburn, the scriptwriter for the "Davy Crockett series," had never before written a song, but that didn't stop him from adding the lyrics, 120 lines of them (the completed version had 20 stanzas of six lines each).

Before the television series even went on the air, "The Ballad of Davy Crockett" took the

Composer George Bruns created a diverse range of music for Disney, from the award-winning score for Sleeping Beauty to the hit song "The Ballad of Davy Crockett."

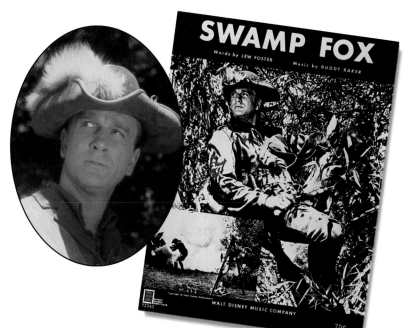

Leslie Nielson not only played the Swamp Fox, but he sang the title song.

country by storm. Bruns and Blackburn's little "throwaway" tune became a monster hit. In the first six months alone, nearly seven million copies of the song were sold, making it the fastest-selling record ever up to that time.

All told, it spent six months on the *Hit Parade*, was recorded by more than 200 record labels around the world and sold an astonishing 10 million copies. Versions of the song were recorded by Bill Hayes (who had the most popular version and the one heard on this collection), Fess Parker (who played Davy Crockett), Tennessee Ernie Ford, Eddie Arnold, Fred Waring, the Sons of the Pioneers, Steve Allen, Mitch Miller, Rusty Draper and Burl Ives.

"It certainly took everybody at the Studio by surprise," said Bruns. "The irony of it was that most people thought it was an authentic folk song that we had uncovered and updated. Usually when you have a hit song, there are always lawsuits claiming prior authorship. In the case of 'Davy Crockett,' not a single suit was filed."

The success of both the show and the song even confounded Walt, who admitted, "We had no idea what was going to happen with Crockett. By the time the show finally got on the air, we were already filming the third one [the series was originally planned as a trilogy] and calmly killing Davy off at the Alamo. The show became one of the biggest overnight hits in TV history, and there we were with just three films and a dead hero."

BUDDY BAKER

In 1954, the music department at the Disney Studio was so busy that George Bruns called in an old friend and former teacher of his to help write the music for the soon-to-premiere "Mickey Mouse Club."

"I came for what I thought would be two weeks' worth of work," says Buddy Baker, "and I stayed 28 years. There was just so much to do I never got a chance to leave."

Baker not only wrote "The Swamp Fox" with lyricist Lew Foster, he also composed and arranged scores for motion pictures, TV series and the Disney theme parks.

"No matter what I or anyone else in the music department wrote, people always recognized it as being the 'Disney sound,' " he says. "But if I was asked to define what the Disney sound is, I'd have to answer that I don't know."

"I think a clue comes from the man himself," he adds. "Walt Disney had a wonderful concept of what the music should be, which is a great clue for a composer. If he wanted a big, symphonic score, he'd tell you that."

When Baker retired from the Disney Studio in 1983, it signaled the end of an era.

"I was the last composer to be on staff at a movie studio," he says. "Nowadays, composers are hired on an 'as needed' basis. They don't actually work for the studios."

Although the real Davy Crockett met a tragic end at the Alamo, the Davy Crockett of TV series fame did not. He rose from the dead and returned the next year in two more shows based on the legends of Davy Crockett, complete with new lyrics to "The Ballad of Davy Crockett" (it was these two shows that were stitched together to make the movie *Davy Crockett and the River Pirates*).

By the way, the original title of "The Ballad of Davy Crockett"— before it became a big hit — was "The Ballad of Davy Crockett: His Early Life, Hunting Adventures, Services Under General Jackson in the Creek War, Electioneering Speeches, Career in Congress, Triumphal Tour in the Northern States, and Services in the Texas War." When that proved to be too difficult to fit on the label of a 78 r.p.m. record, it was shortened.

Long before Lt. Frank Dreben and *The Naked Gun*, there was General Francis Marion and *The Swamp Fox*. The link between the two is actor Leslie Nielsen, who in 1959 starred as General Marion in Disney's miniseries about American revolutionaries who took to the swamps of South Carolina to battle British troops.

The real treat of each episode, which was seen as part of Disney's weekly TV show (by that time renamed "Walt Disney Presents") was

49

Leslie Nielsen and sidekick Jordan Whitfield in The Swamp Fox.

Guy Williams in Zorro *avenges the downtrodden — complete with a recognizable mask and a theme song.*

anthology show. Both became motion pictures that were assembled by editing together several episodes of their TV shows. And both shared George Bruns as the composer of their theme songs.

"Zorro," with music by Bruns and words by Norman Foster, was heard for the two seasons the show was on ABC and then popped up again later when "Zorro" was revived as a series of one-hour episodes for Walt Disney's weekly TV show and as a motion picture in 1960.

In 1990 Disney reentered the realm of daily children's television with "The Disney Afternoon," a two-hour block of cartoons starring both classic and new Disney characters. The original lineup included "DuckTales," "Chip 'n Dale's Rescue Rangers," "Disney's Adventures of the Gummi Bears" and "Tale Spin." By 1991, all four shows were among the six top-rated animated shows in syndicated television. Not surprisingly, all feature bouncy, irresistible theme songs that are as easily identified by today's generation of kids as "The Mickey Mouse Club March" was to yesterday's. The two themes on this collection are the **"DuckTales Theme"** and the **"Tale Spin Theme."**

hearing Nielsen sing **"The Swamp Fox,"** with words by Lew Foster and music by Buddy Baker.

In 1968 "Walt Disney's Wonderful World of Color" became "The Wonderful World of Disney" and received a new theme song, titled, appropriately enough, **"The Wonderful World of Disney (Main Title)."** Actually, the new theme song was a medley of Disney's greatest hits. Can you identify them?

(Answer: "Someday My Prince Will Come," "Whistle While You Work," "When You Wish Upon a Star," "Chim Chim Cher-ee," "Zip-A-Dee-Doo-Dah," "The Ballad of Davy Crockett" and "Bibbidi-Bobbidi-Boo.")

In 1957, a Spanish Californian aristocrat who doubles as a masked avenger came galloping into America's homes. Although "Zorro" didn't quite cause the same sensation as the "Davy Crockett" shows did, there are similarities between the two. Both started out on TV, "Zorro" as a weekly series, "Crockett" as a mini-series on Disney's weekly

Classic Disney characters join a new team in "The Disney Afternoon."

A Song In The Parks

To Walt Disney, the creation of a theme park was the next logical step for a man who had spent most of his life making movies.

In many ways, his "magical little park," as he called it, would be just like the movies. It would have stories, themes, sets, action, dialogue, humor, drama, happy endings and, of course, music.

But there would be one very important difference. At Disneyland people would feel as if they were actually walking into the movies. Instead of just sitting in a darkened theater vicariously enjoying a motion picture up on a screen, they would be right in the middle of it with the action unfolding all around them.

Not surprisingly, Walt was very conscious of what music would be played in Disneyland. The soundtrack for the park would be just as

"Disneyland is like Alice stepping through the Looking Glass. To step through the portals of Disneyland will be like entering another world."

Walt Disney

Music would be an integral part of the Disneyland experience

important as the score for a motion picture. The only difference was that Disneyland would have many scores. Each land would have one, as would most of the attractions. Even some of the shops and restaurants would have their own musical variations.

And then, of course, there were the songs. As in a musical motion picture, they would be an integral part of the Disneyland experience, advancing and in some cases even telling the story that goes along with an attraction.

Some of the music was simply adapted from the films to the theme park. For instance, "The Unbirthday Song" is heard at the *Mad Tea Party* and "You Can Fly! You Can Fly! You Can Fly!" provides the background for *Peter Pan's Flight*.

There are also a few obscure songs from Disney films that have been adapted or arranged for Disneyland. The melody for **"Meet Me Down on Main Street,"** which has served as the unofficial theme song for Main Street, U.S.A. since the mid-1950s, had its origins in the 1950 Donald Duck cartoon *Crazy Over Daisy*. In the short, Donald plays a Gay '90s beau trying to woo the ever-elusive Daisy Duck; hence, the turn-of-the-century melody and feel.

Tom Adair and Disney music director Oliver Wallace are credited as the writers of the song, which was released as a single by a barbershop

Fireworks light the sky over Sleeping Beauty Castle *at Disneyland.*

quartet called the Mellomen in the late 1950s (it's their version that is heard on this collection).

But there have been many songs written especially for the Disneyland and Walt Disney World theme parks. Several of them were written in the 1960s when a certain pair of brothers were working as staff songwriters for the Disney Studio. So, take a wild guess as to who those brothers are.

Did you guess the Sherman brothers? Not surprisingly, Richard and Robert Sherman proved to be just as effective (and prolific) writing songs for Disneyland as they did penning them for Disney films and TV shows.

One such tune was a theme song for an Adventureland attraction that features singing birds, flowers and tikis. *The Enchanted Tiki Room* opened at Disneyland in 1963 and was the first to use the *Audio-Animatronics*® system creating realistic-looking animated figures that move, talk and sing.

The Shermans wrote a bouncy little song for the *Tiki Room* called — what else?— **"The Tiki Tiki Tiki Room,"** that's filled with shameless puns and groaning one-liners, but it's the

52

type of song that's so irresistibly infectious that people end up walking out of the attraction humming it.

Another Sherman brothers song that's eminently hummable (and even that's an understatement) wasn't actually written for an attraction at Disneyland.

It came about when Walt was in the process of putting together an attraction for UNICEF for the 1964-65 New York World's Fair. One day he asked the brothers to look at a mock-up of the exhibit, which featured mechanical figures in native costumes from around the world, each singing their respective national anthem.

"The idea and the animation were great," said Richard Sherman, "but what a cacophony of sound."

"That's the problem," he recalled Walt as saying. "I want you guys to come up with a simple little song that has the idea of spirit and brotherly love and goodwill... and can you write it fast?"

The Shermans did, coming up with **"It's a Small World (After All),"** which debuted at the New York World's Fair and quickly became a worldwide phenomenon. Since that time, the attraction and the song have opened at Disneyland, the Magic Kingdom at Walt Disney World, Tokyo Disneyland and most recently at

(Above) Happy children from around the world sing a hopeful anthem in It's a Small World. *(Right) Music plays a key role in one of Disney's grandest attractions —* Pirates of the Caribbean.

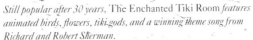

Still popular after 30 years, The Enchanted Tiki Room *features animated birds, flowers, tiki-gods, and a winning theme song from Richard and Robert Sherman.*

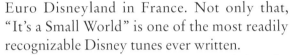

The song that linked the scenes in Carousel of Progress *was "There's a Great Big Beautiful Tomorrow," said to be the Shermans' tribute to the spirit of Walt Disney.*

Euro Disneyland in France. Not only that, "It's a Small World" is one of the most readily recognizable Disney tunes ever written.

Another pavilion Disney created for the 1964-65 New York World's Fair was the *Carousel of Progress.* Sponsored by General Electric, the show was designed to demonstrate the ways electricity and modern conveniences had improved the quality of people's lives.

Walt needed a song to bridge the changes in scenes so, as usual, he turned to the Sherman brothers, who responded with **"There's a Great Big Beautiful Tomorrow."**

After it had finished its run at the World's Fair, Walt decided to make some changes in the show and move it to Disneyland. The "new and improved" version, which opened in 1967, featured improved *Audio-Animatronics* figures and a more sophisticated "moving" carousel

theater in which the audience revolved from scene to scene.

When the *Carousel of Progress* moved to Walt Disney World in 1973, "There's a Great Big Beautiful Tomorrow" was retired (replaced by another Sherman brothers song, "The Best Time of Your Life"). However, it received a new lease on life in 1983 when it became a featured song at *Horizons* at EPCOT Center in the Walt Disney World resort.

Despite what you may be thinking, the Sherman brothers weren't the only ones writing songs for Disney during the 1960s. George Bruns, the composer responsible for scoring such films as *Sleeping Beauty* and writing such hits as "The Ballad of Davy Crockett," was also quite prolific during this period and he, too, tried his hand at writing a song or two for Disneyland.

One of the most recognizable, in which he teamed with Disney Imagineer Xavier Atencio, is **"Yo, Ho (A Pirate's Life for Me),"** written for *Pirates of the Caribbean,* which opened at Disneyland in 1967.

Atencio, a longtime Disney employee who helped create the nursery sequence in *Mary Poppins,* not only wrote the lyrics to "Yo, Ho," he also wrote the script for the attraction.

53

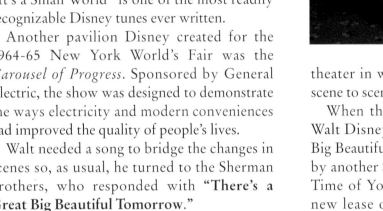

MAIN
STREET
ELECTRICAL
PARADE

Disneyland and the Magic Kingdom at Walt Disney World aren't the only Disney theme parks to have songs written for their lands, shows and attractions. When EPCOT Center opened in 1982, it boasted more than a dozen new tunes written by a new generation of Disney songwriters. One of those songs is **"Golden Dream,"** heard at *The American Adventure* in World Showcase.

Written by Bob Moline (who wrote several other EPCOT songs, as well) with lyrics by the attraction's producer and scriptwriter Randy Bright, "Golden Dream" was arranged and conducted by longtime Disney composer Buddy Baker using the Philadelphia Orchestra. The vocals are by Marti McCall and Richard Page.

Certainly one of the most popular songs heard at the Disney theme parks over the years is **"Baroque Hoedown,"** a song better known as the theme to the Main Street Electrical Parade. Written by Jean Jacques Perry and Gershon Kingsley, the song is performed entirely on synthesizers.

So there it is, over 60 years of Disney music, from animated features and live-action movies to television series and theme park attractions. It seems only fitting that for the last word about *The Music of Disney: A Legacy in Song,* we turn to Walt Disney himself:

"Music has always had a prominent part in all our products from the early cartoon days. So much so, in fact, that I cannot think of the pictorial story without thinking about the complementary music that will fulfill it... I have had no formal musical training. But by long experience and by strong personal leaning, I've selected musical themes, original or adapted, that were guided to wide audience acceptance.

"But credit for the memorable songs and scores must, of course, go to the brilliant composers and musicians who have been associated with me through the years."

(Left) At EPCOT Center, Mark Twain and Ben Franklin host The American Adventure, *which concludes with the inspiring song, "Golden Dream."*

"I cannot think of the pictorial story without thinking about the complementary music that will fulfill it."

Song Index

One

Turkey in the Straw
Steamboat Willie (1928)
Traditional

Who's Afraid of the Big Bad Wolf?**
Three Little Pigs (1933)
Vocals: Pinto Colvig, Mary Moder, Dorothy Compton and Billy Bletcher
Words and Music by Frank Churchill and Ann Ronell

Heigh-Ho**
Snow White and the Seven Dwarfs (1937)
Vocals: The Dwarf Chorus
Words and Music by Larry Morey and Frank Churchill

Whistle While You Work**
Snow White and the Seven Dwarfs (1937)
Lead Vocal: Adriana Caselotti
Words and Music by Larry Morey and Frank Churchill

Someday My Prince Will Come**
Snow White and the Seven Dwarfs (1937)
Lead Vocal: Adriana Caselotti
Words and Music by Larry Morey and Frank Churchill

When You Wish Upon a Star**
Pinocchio (1940)
Lead Vocal: Cliff Edwards
Words and Music by Ned Washington and Leigh Harline

Give a Little Whistle**
Pinocchio (1940)
Vocals: Cliff Edwards and Dickie Jones
Words and Music by Ned Washington and Leigh Harline

Dance of the Reed Flutes
Fantasia (1940)
Performed by the Philadelphia Orchestra
Music by Peter Ilich Tchaikovsky
Conducted by Leopold Stokowski

Baby Mine††
Dumbo (1941)
Lead Vocal: Betty Noyes
Words and Music by Ned Washington and Frank Churchill

Love Is a Song†
Bambi (1942)
Lead Vocal: Donald Novis
Words and Music by Larry Morey and Frank Churchill

Little April Shower†
Bambi (1942)
Vocals: Amy Lou Barnes, Sally Mueller, Mary Moder,
Alice Sizer and Betty Bruce
Words and Music by Larry Morey and Frank Churchill

Saludos Amigos*
Saludos Amigos (1943)
Vocals: Disney Studio Chorus
Words and Music by Ned Washington and Charles Wolcott

You Belong to My Heart*†*
The Three Caballeros (1944)
Lead Vocal: Dora Luz
Words and Music by Agustin Lara and Ray Gilbert

Zip-A-Dee-Doo-Dah*
Song of the South (1946)
Lead Vocal: James Baskett
Words and Music by Ray Gilbert and Allie Wrubel

Ev'rybody Has a Laughing Place*
Song of the South (1946)
Vocals: James Baskett, Jesse Cryor, Johnny Lee and Nicodemus Stewart
Words and Music by Ray Gilbert and Allie Wrubel

The Lord Is Good to Me*
Melody Time (1948)
Lead Vocal: Dennis Day
Words and Music by Kim Gannon and Walter Kent

Lavender Blue (Dilly, Dilly)*
So Dear to My Heart (1949)
Lead Vocal: Burl Ives
Words and Music by Larry Morey and Eliot Daniel

A Dream Is a Wish Your Heart Makes*
Cinderella (1950)
Lead Vocal: Ilene Woods
Words and Music by Mack David, Al Hoffman and Jerry Livingston

Bibbidi-Bobbidi-Boo*
Cinderella (1950)
Lead Vocals: Verna Felton, Ilene Woods and James Macdonald
Words and Music by Jerry Livingston, Mack David and Al Hoffman

I'm Late*
Alice in Wonderland (1951)
Vocals: Bill Thompson and Kathryn Beaumont
Words and Music by Bob Hilliard and Sammy Fain

The Unbirthday Song*
Alice in Wonderland (1951)
Vocals: Jerry Colonna, Ed Wynn and Kathryn Beaumont
Words and Music by Mack David, Al Hoffman and Jerry Livingston

The Second Star to the Right*
Peter Pan (1953)
Vocals: The Jud Conlon Chorus
Words and Music by Sammy Cahn and Sammy Fain

You Can Fly! You Can Fly! You Can Fly!*
Peter Pan (1953)
Lead Vocals: Bobby Driscoll, Kathryn Beaumont,
Paul Collins and Tommy Luske
Words and Music by Sammy Cahn and Sammy Fain

Bella Notte*
Lady and the Tramp (1955)
Lead Vocals: Bill Hamlin and Oliver Wallace
Words and Music by Peggy Lee and Sonny Burke

Once Upon a Dream*
Sleeping Beauty (1959)
Lead Vocals: Mary Costa and Bill Shirley
Words and Music by Jack Lawrence and Sammy Fain
Based on the theme by Peter Ilich Tchaikovsky

Cruella De Vil*
101 Dalmatians (1961)
Vocals: Bill Lee, Lisa Davis and Ben Wright
Words and Music by Mel Leven

Higitus Figitus†
The Sword in the Stone (1963)
Vocals: Karl Swensen and Ricky Sorenson
Words and Music by Richard M. Sherman and Robert B. Sherman

** 1933, 1937, 1940 Bourne Co. (ASCAP). Copyright renewed.
†† 1941 Walt Disney Productions (ASCAP). World rights controlled by
Bourne Co. Copyright renewed.
* 1943, 1945, 1946, 1948, 1949, 1951, 1952, 1954, 1961
Walt Disney Music Company (ASCAP). Copyright renewed.
† 1942, 1962 Wonderland Music Company, Inc. (BMI). Copyright renewed.
† 1943 Peer International Corporation (BMI). Copyright renewed.

Two

Supercalifragilisticexpialidocious†
Mary Poppins (1964)
Vocals: Julie Andrews, Dick Van Dyke and The Pearlie Chorus featuring
Richard M. Sherman and J. Pat O'Malley
Words and Music by Richard M. Sherman and Robert B. Sherman

A Spoonful of Sugar†
Mary Poppins (1964)
Lead Vocal: Julie Andrews
Words and Music by Richard M. Sherman and Robert B. Sherman

Chim Chim Cher-ee†
Mary Poppins (1964)
Vocals: Dick Van Dyke, Julie Andrews, Karen Dotrice and Matthew Garber
Words and Music by Richard M. Sherman and Robert B. Sherman

Winnie the Pooh†
Winnie the Pooh and the Honey Tree (1966)
Vocals: Disney Studio Chorus
Words and Music by Richard M. Sherman and Robert B. Sherman

The Bare Necessities†
The Jungle Book (1967)
Vocals: Phil Harris and Bruce Reitherman
Words and Music by Terry Gilkyson

I Wan'na Be Like You†
The Jungle Book (1967)
Vocals: Louis Prima, Phil Harris and Bruce Reitherman
Words and Music by Richard M. Sherman and Robert B. Sherman

The Aristocats*
The Aristocats (1970)
Lead Vocal: Maurice Chevalier
Words and Music by Richard M. Sherman and Robert B. Sherman

Ev'rybody Wants to Be a Cat*
The Aristocats (1970)
Vocals: Phil Harris, Scatman Crothers, Thurl Ravenscroft and Liz English
Words and Music by Floyd Huddleston and Al Rinker

The Age of Not Believing†
Bedknobs and Broomsticks (1971)
Lead Vocal: Angela Lansbury
Words and Music by Richard M. Sherman and Robert B. Sherman

Nobody's Problems†
Bedknobs and Broomsticks (1971)
(Demo recording)
Lead Vocal: Angela Lansbury
Words and Music by Richard M. Sherman and Robert B. Sherman
Piano Accompaniment: Irwin Kostal

Oo-De-Lally†
Robin Hood (1973)
Lead Vocal: Roger Miller
Words and Music by Roger Miller

Someone's Waiting for You*
The Rescuers (1977)
Lead Vocal: Shelby Flint
Words and Music by Carol Connors, Ayn Robbins and Sammy Fain

Candle on the Water**
Pete's Dragon (1977)
Lead Vocal: Helen Reddy
Words and Music by Al Kasha and Joel Hirschhorn

Best of Friends†*
The Fox and the Hound (1981)
Lead Vocal: Pearl Bailey
Words and Music by Stan Fidel and Richard Johnston

Perfect Isn't Easy†
Oliver & Company (1988)
Lead Vocal: Bette Midler
Words and Music by Jack Feldman, Bruce Sussman and Barry Manilow

Part of Your World†⁑
The Little Mermaid (1989)
Lead Vocal: Jodi Benson
Words and Music by Howard Ashman and Alan Menken

Under the Sea†⁑
The Little Mermaid (1989)
Lead Vocal: Samuel E. Wright
Words and Music by Howard Ashman and Alan Menken

Kiss the Girl⁑
The Little Mermaid (1989)
Lead Vocal: Samuel E. Wright
Words and Music by Howard Ashman and Alan Menken

Be Our Guest†⁑
Beauty and the Beast (1991)
Lead Vocals: Jerry Orbach and Angela Lansbury
Words and Music by Howard Ashman and Alan Menken

Beauty and the Beast†⁑
Beauty and the Beast (1991)
Vocals: Angela Lansbury
Words and Music by Howard Ashman and Alan Menken

Three

A Whale of a Tale†
20,000 Leagues Under the Sea (1954)
Lead Vocal: Kirk Douglas
Words and Music by Al Hoffman and Norman Gimbel

Old Yeller⁂
Old Yeller (1957)
Lead Vocal: Jerome Courtland
Words and Music by Gil George and Oliver Wallace

Pretty Irish Girl⁂
Darby O'Gill and the Little People (1959)
(Demo recording)
Lead Vocal: Sean Connery
Words and Music by Larry Watkin and Oliver Wallace

The Parent Trap†
The Parent Trap (1961)
Vocals: Tommy Sands and Annette Funicello
Words and Music by Richard M. Sherman and Robert B. Sherman

Castle in Spain⁂
Babes in Toyland (1961)
Lead Vocal: Ray Bolger
Words and Music by Mel Leven and George Bruns
Based on the music by Victor Herbert

Enjoy It†
In Search of the Castaways (1962)
Vocals: Maurice Chevalier and Hayley Mills
Words and Music by Richard M. Sherman and Robert B. Sherman

On the Front Porch†
Summer Magic (1963)
Lead Vocal: Burl Ives
Words and Music by Richard M. Sherman and Robert B. Sherman

The Monkey's Uncle†
The Monkey's Uncle (1965)
Lead Vocal: Annette Funicello
Words and Music by Richard M. Sherman and Robert B. Sherman

That Darn Cat†
That Darn Cat (1965)
Lead Vocal: Bobby Troup
Words and Music by Richard M. Sherman and Robert B. Sherman

Fortuosity†
The Happiest Millionaire (1967)
Lead Vocal: Tommy Steele
Words and Music by Richard M. Sherman and Robert B. Sherman

Mickey Mouse Club March⁂
The Mickey Mouse Club (1955)
Lead Vocals: The Mouseketeers
Words and Music by Jimmie Dodd

I'm No Fool⁂
The Mickey Mouse Club (1956)
Lead Vocal: Cliff Edwards
Words and Music by Jimmie Dodd

You, the Human Animal⁂
The Mickey Mouse Club (1956)
Lead Vocal: Cliff Edwards
Words and Music by Jimmie Dodd

Mickey Mouse Club Alma Mater⁂
The Mickey Mouse Club (1955)
Vocals: The Mouseketeers and Jimmie Dodd
Words and Music by Jimmie Dodd

Wonderful World of Color (Main Title)†
Walt Disney's Wonderful World of Color (1961)
Vocals: The Wellingtons
Words and Music by Richard M. Sherman and Robert B. Sherman

The Spectrum Song†
Walt Disney's Wonderful World of Color (1961)
Vocal: Paul Frees
Words and Music by Richard M. Sherman and Robert B. Sherman

The Ballad of Davy Crockett†
Davy Crockett (1955)
Vocals: The Mellomen
Words and Music by Tom Blackburn and George Bruns

The Swamp Fox⁂
The Swamp Fox (1959)
Lead Vocal: Leslie Nielsen
Words and Music by Lew Foster and Buddy Baker

The Wonderful World of Disney (Main Title)⁂
The Wonderful World of Disney (1968)
Music and Arrangement by George Bruns

Zorro⁂
Zorro (1957)
Vocals: The Mellomen
Words and Music by Norman Foster and George Bruns

Strummin' Song†
Walt Disney's Wonderful World of Color (1961)
Lead Vocal: Annette Funicello
Words and Music by Richard M. Sherman and Robert B. Sherman

Mister Piano Man†
Golden Horseshoe Review (1962)
Lead Vocal: Annette Funicello
Words and Music by Richard M. Sherman and Robert B. Sherman

DuckTales Theme†
DuckTales (1990)
Lead Vocal: Jeff Pescetto
Words and Music by Mark Mueller

Tale Spin Theme†
Tale Spin (1990)
Vocals: Jim Gilstrap
Words and Music by Michael Silversher and Patty Silversher

Meet Me Down on Main Street⁂
Disneyland (1956)
Vocals: The Mellomen
Words and Music by Tom Adair and Oliver Wallace

The Tiki, Tiki, Tiki Room†
Disneyland (1963)
Vocals: Wally Boag, Fulton Burley, Thurl Ravenscroft and The Mellomen
Words and Music by Richard M. Sherman and Robert B. Sherman

It's a Small World (After All)†
New York World's Fair (1964)
Vocals: The Disneyland Chorus
Words and Music by Richard M. Sherman and Robert B. Sherman

Yo, Ho (A Pirate's Life for Me)⁂
Disneyland (1967)
Vocals: The Mellomen
Words and Music by Xavier Atencio and George Bruns

There's a Great Big Beautiful Tomorrow†
New York World's Fair (1964)
Lead Vocal: Rex Allen
Words and Music by Richard M. Sherman and Robert B. Sherman

Golden Dream⁂
EPCOT Center (1982)
Lead Vocals: Richard Page and Marti McCall
Words and Music by Randy Bright and Bob Moline

Main Street Electrical Parade†††
Disneyland (1979)
Theme by Jean Jacques Perrey and Gershon Kingsley

Music Compilation

Compilation produced by Michael Leon
Additional production by Ron Kidd, Ted Kryczko and Randy Thornton
Executive Producer: Harold J. Kleiner
Audio research: Bambi Moé, Ron Moortgat, Les Perkins, Paula Sigman and Jack Wadsworth
Digitally remastered by Ted Hall at Digital Magnetics, Hollywood, CA

Collector's Book

Written by David J. Fisher
Edited by Christine Goosman
Editorial supervision by Greg Dobrin
Art direction and graphic design by Vince Peterson in collaboration with Ridgley Curry & Associates Inc.
Production supervision by Johanna Leovey
Photography by Michael Stern and Paul Ottengheime
Cover image: photography by Paul Ottengheime; illustration by Ron Dias
Additional research by David Tietyen and Kevin A. Sinclair
Archive photos provided by the Walt Disney Photo Library
Disney memorabilia provided by the Walt Disney Archives and the private "Disneyana" collection of Willie Ito

Special thanks to Stacia Martin of Disneyland, Les Perkins of Disney Character Voices, Paula Sigman of Disney Collectibles, David R. Smith and Robert Tieman of the Walt Disney Archives and Jeanette Steiner of the Disney Publishing Group.